05-09

BPD-35995 © 2003 Antioch Publishing

THIS BOOK BELONGS TO

A. Dale Crain

714-847-3446

THE POLITICS OF DISASTER
KATRINA, BIG GOVERNMENT, AND A NEW STRATEGY
FOR FUTURE CRISES

OTHER BOOKS BY MARVIN OLASKY

THE POLITICS OF DISASTER
KATRINA, BIG GOVERNMENT, AND A NEW STRATEGY FOR FUTURE CRISES

MARVIN OLASKY

W PUBLISHING GROUP
A Division of Thomas Nelson Publishers
Since 1798

Published by W Publishing Group®, a division of Thomas Nelson, Inc., P.O. Box 141000, Nashville, Tennessee 37214.

W Publishing Group books may be purchased in bulk for educational, business, fund-raising, or sales promotional use. For information, please e-mail SpecialMarkets@ThomasNelson.com.

Cover Design: Don Bailey
Page Design: Mandi Cofer

ISBN 0-8499-0172-3

Printed in the United States of America

For Susan, more lovely than ever
after thirty years of marriage

CONTENTS

INTRODUCTION

We act as if we're immune. We build below sea level, or on barrier islands, or on hillsides with brush that annually burns, or over earthquake faults—and we're shocked, shocked when disasters occur. We use levee repair funds to build parkways or spruce up gambling casinos, and we're shocked when old levees give way.

We think that if we have well-built houses we're immune. British colonials had grand homes in Calcutta, but their roofs came off and many of their walls fell in when a cyclone struck the port on October 5, 1864. The cyclone also blew away rickety native huts as if they were twigs: eighty thousand died from the wind and the forty-foot-high wall of water it created.

We think that if we build big, strong buildings we're immune. In the 1988 Armenian earthquake, the 1995 Japanese earthquake, and the 1999 Turkish earthquake, new multistoried buildings—including ones that conformed to California's Uniform Building Code—collapsed. Japan's calamity left fifty-five hundred dead and was, according to a subsequent risk management report, "a terribly striking example of what earthquakes can do to a modern industrialized society."

We think that with enough warning we're immune. However, San Franciscans knew that an earthquake was coming, and New Orleans residents knew that a hurricane was coming. Many people over the years have had volcanoes as neighbors. Mount Krakatoa in Indonesia began erupting in May 1883, three months before its enormous explosion killed thirty-six thousand, but undisturbed residents even climbed to the volcano's peak to peer inside. Six years later in Johnstown, Pennsylvania, residents had a running joke that "the dam has burst; take to the hills." When it did break, there was little time to run, so twenty-five hundred died.

Some people in New Orleans who thought, or hoped, that the city was immune behind its levees should have read about the city's 1927 flood or about how the Yangtze River flood in 1954 killed forty thousand and left one million people homeless. The United States had planned to build the world's largest dam on the Yangtze River, for both power and flood control, but China's new Communist government used clay soil to build levees that collapsed, submerging an area twice the size of Texas.

Disasters happen, but the number of fatalities increases when short-term goals take precedence over long-term safety. Before Mount Pelee erupted on the French island of Martinique in the West Indies on May 8, 1902, residents of the nearby city of St. Pierre smelled sulfur fumes for weeks. Compared to Martinique officials, Louisiana's recent leaders seem like geniuses. The governor in St. Pierre did not want anything to get in the way of his May 10 reelection, so he set up roadblocks to keep constituents from leaving before they could cast ballots. The local newspaper mocked those who worried. Its editor, along with forty thousand other residents, died during the eruption.

Building houses below sea level or along a hurricane-hit shore makes as much sense as the southern European practice, during the eighteenth and nineteenth centuries, of using church vaults to store gunpowder. Churches had steeples or bell towers susceptible to lightning strikes: a lightning strike, fire, and subsequent gunpowder explosion in Brescia, Italy, in 1769 killed three thousand people. A similar lightning strike and explosion on the island of Rhodes in 1856 killed four thousand.

Unanticipated problems are inevitable, but politics and pride can turn them into disasters. In 1912 some fifteen hundred died when the "unsinkable" *Titanic* sunk on its first transatlantic voyage, in part because of a prideful lack of concern about icebergs and in part because of a technical flaw: the separating walls in its "watertight" compartments did not extend all the way to the top, so the water flowed from one to the next. Two years later, one thousand voyagers died on the St. Lawrence River when the *Empress of Ireland*, going too fast amid fog, slammed into a coaling ship. These were not acts of God. They were acts of men.

Why do such disasters happen? Thousands of books and articles have tackled the subject of theodicy, asking whether catastrophes disprove the belief that God exists and that He is good: at the end of 2005, Google showed 275,000 mentions of "theodicy." "Anthropodicy," the question of whether man acts rightly (and whether "human intelligence" is an oxymoron), garnered only 145 mentions. Our tendency to put God rather than ourselves on trial is evident.

In 1946 the Winecoff Hotel in Atlanta, after running ads announcing it was "Absolutely Fire Proof," caught fire and 119 died. Twelve-inch-thick brick walls made the structure fireproof, but everything inside burned. The fifteen-story hotel had no fire alarm or sprinkler system, no fire escapes or fire doors, just one spiral staircase plus elevators. An act of man, surely.

Hurricanes, earthquakes, and the like are acts of God. The extent of the damage they cause often depends on the politics and economics of man. That goes for good news as well as bad. When Hurricane Fifi wreaked havoc in Honduras in 1974, widespread starvation ensued. Yet when Hurricane Katrina destroyed homes, a robust American economy kept famine from being a fear. Still, we are not immune to natural catastrophe, terrorist-caused disaster, and the unnatural amplification of both.

In one sense, personal disasters surround us. Every ten seconds in the United States a person is injured in a motor vehicle accident. Every twenty-six seconds a person has a heart attack. Every fifty-seven seconds a person dies from cancer. But this book examines incidents, some partially preventable, that have a major negative impact on the ability of an entire community to live peaceably. Some disasters, like hurricanes or earthquakes, are suddenly explosive. Others, like pandemics or the plagues of terrorism or revolutionary bloodletting, may start slowly and conclude with prolonged whimpering.

This book examines the politics of disaster in six parts, each with three chapters. Using the Hurricane Katrina disaster as a case study, part 1 details what went wrong with government and media responses to Hurricane Katrina and explains how those problems were part of a long trend in disaster responses. Part 2 describes what went right by assessing the work of three Katrina responders that were effective: business, the military, and religious groups.

Part 3 proposes a reconceptualization of how we respond to disaster and suggests specific public policy measures based on our experience. Part 4 looks in detail at the role of faith-based organizations in disaster response. Part 5 examines several recent disasters abroad and the effectiveness of key responders in meeting the challenges. Part 6 examines three disasters that many believe are likely to occur in the United States sometime during the coming decades—a California earthquake, nuclear terrorism, and a pandemic—and assesses how prepared we are to respond.

We'll be investigating some new and frightening developments, but it's important to remember that disasters aren't new. Brimstone buried Sodom and Gomorrah about four thousand years ago, and an earthquake about three hundred years later brought the Minoan civilization on Crete to an end. Greek philosophers such as Plato knew about disaster: an earthquake and tidal wave buried the Greek city of Helike in 373 BC. In AD 79 medieval disasters destroyed cities such as Dunwich, England, and Rungholt, Germany. The 1755 Lisbon earthquake became a propagandistic windfall for Voltaire.

Nor is the way we respond entirely new. The National Academy of Public Administration, in 1993, expressed concern about the "CNN Syndrome": "Disaster and emergencies provide dramatic news and the appetites of news media, particularly television, are insatiable. . . . [Disasters] will now be 'nationalized' and politicized as a result of media coverage. . . . The media pressure reluctant local and state leaders to 'ask for federal help,' presidents to dispatch such help, and representatives and senators to demand it on behalf of their constituents." That's all true, but when Mount Vesuvius exploded in AD 79 and covered Pompeii and Herculaneum with molten ash, messengers reported the horror, Romans clamored for relief to be sent, and Emperor Titus complied.

Media move much more quickly now and make news of suffering immediate, but most Americans still don't take the precaution of always having several days of food and water on hand. Rebecca O'Connor, in December 2005, wrote in the *Los Angeles Times*: "[I] took a good look in my pantry yesterday. I have enough soup and refried beans to last two days. There's a six-pack of water and a half a box of crackers, both of which would be gone by tomorrow if something happened today. I have no spare batteries, which isn't a problem because I don't own a battery-operated radio. . . . I live right smack between two active fault lines. A devastating earthquake is inevitable here in somebody's lifetime. Still, I just can't bring myself to stock my shelves. . . . I surely believe in natural disasters. I just don't believe they'll happen to me."

While we act as if we are immune from disaster, governmental policies now normalize it. Just as insurance now covers regular dental checkups, disaster designation now covers thoroughly predictable events such as blizzards. The first president with the power to issue a declaration of disaster, Dwight Eisenhower, issued 107 such declarations during his eight years in office, an average of thirteen per year. That rose to an annual average of eighteen during the Kennedy/Johnson years and more than doubled to an average of thirty-seven during the Nixon/Ford administrations.

Engineer Jimmy Carter, trying to rein in the excesses, averaged thirty-two declarations of disaster or emergency per year. Budget-conscious Ronald Reagan reduced the average to twenty-eight. But the number jumped under George H. W. Bush, who averaged forty-three declarations during each of his four years, and it was off to the races with Bill Clinton, who more than doubled the total to eighty-eight. George W. Bush has been even more promiscuous in his declarations: during his first five years in office he averaged 139 per year, or one every 2.6 days.

A further dive into the numbers shows that they peak in presidential election years, and that's not just coincidence. Two researchers, Mary W. Downton of the National Center for Atmospheric Research and Roger A. Pielke Jr. of the University of Colorado, Boulder, took into account the amount of precipitation each year as they examined flood-related disasters from 1965 to 1997 and found that the average number of flood-related disasters declared by the president in election years was 46 percent higher than it should have been.

Two other researchers, Thomas A. Garrett and Russell S. Sobel, concluded that congressional as well as presidential politics have an effect on disaster declarations. Controlling statistically for the damage caused by storms from 1991 to 1999, they found a correlation between disaster relief dollars and the number of representatives a state has on the two major Federal Emergency Management Agency oversight committees in the House of Representatives: each additional representative on one of those committees brought an extra $36.5 million of assistance from FEMA. Overall, one-third of FEMA payments seemed directly attributable to representation on one of the nine FEMA congressional oversight committees, regardless of a disaster's severity.

The result is not just budget busting but amplification of the already existing tendency of Americans to become subjects rather than citizens, dependently waiting for federal money rather than independently acting. That leads to atrophy of local and state muscles. The availability of funds from Washington leads people to ask what this country can do for them, instead of what they can do for themselves and for their neighbors.

And as poor welfare recipients have learned over the years, middle-class Americans, who are the main recipients of disaster aid, grow to despise the hand that feeds them but also points them toward stacks of paper. As one housing official said after the 1989 California earthquake, "Middle class people are not used to standing in endless lines to get a government hand-out," and they are angry when told to do so. Meanwhile, congresspeople tend to hate disasters rhetorically but love them politically—they are not forced to cut anything, and many of their constituents benefit, even prosper.

But this is far from a victimless political crime. The likelihood of a federal bailout often leads to reduced caution on the part of local residents and owners. Governmental compassion enables people to love a piece of property and lose it, then receive sufficient compensation for them to love and lose again and again. From a budgetary standpoint, it is not better to have materially loved and lost than never to have loved at all. When the process becomes repetitive, it becomes insane.

Is there a way out? This is one of the questions we will explore.

Part One

WHAT WENT WRONG IN NEW ORLEANS?

Despite the leadership failures and journalistic misreporting that this section will describe, the federal response to the New Orleans disaster occurred in seventy-two to ninety-six hours as FEMA planned—but reporters and politicians were furious after forty-eight. New Orleans Homeland Security director Terry Ebbert had said, before the hurricane hit, that survival was at stake, so "I'm not worried about what is tolerable or intolerable. I'm worried about whether you are alive." Several days later, as the *New York Times* reported, Ebbert was lambasting the federal government: "It's criminal within the confines of the United States that within one hour of the hurricane they weren't force-feeding us."

The federal government also produced its share of over-the-top statements. The headline of a FEMA press release on August 29, 2005, the day Katrina came ashore, was "First Responders Urged Not to Respond to Hurricane Impact Areas Unless Dispatched by State, Local Authorities."

That top-down understanding might have made theoretical sense in conjunction with FEMA's statement that "the National Incident Management System is being used during the response to Hurricane Katrina and that self-dispatching volunteer assistance could significantly complicate the response and recovery effort." But that system quickly proved inadequate, and FEMA justly received ridicule for going by the book even as high winds were ripping out its pages.

Given that experience and the American emphasis on separation of powers, we are unlikely to see federal force-feeding during future disasters. Enforcement of a truly comprehensive plan requires a czar, and Americans are reluctant to toss out our heritage of individualistic action, even in emergencies. Besides, planners can never fully anticipate the inevitable complexity of events, so even if we do not repeat mistakes, we have the opportunity to make new ones. Pity the officials who make false steps at a time when litigation looms. The ever-present threat of lawsuits makes moot the old debate about whether the United States is a republic or a democracy: the United States is now a paperocracy.

Chapter 1

KATRINA'S PAPEROCRACY

In the immediate aftermath of Hurricane Katrina, some said the New Orleans problem was lack of planning. Then the truth emerged: at least three different bureaucracies had produced lots of plans. They had all succumbed to rule by paperocracy.

The city of New Orleans's "Comprehensive Emergency Disaster Plan" was not comprehensive enough to call for the evacuation of the sick, the elderly, and the poor. The state of Louisiana's comprehensive plan assumed movement of New Orleans residents to shelters outside New Orleans. The Federal Emergency Management Agency's comprehensive plan was based on national disaster standards that tell local and state officials not to expect federal aid for three or four days. Until then FEMA wanted residents to depend on themselves and on local leaders, with a disciplined police force responsible for preventing looting and assault.

The intent was to cross-pollinate these plans to create something truly comprehensive, but that wasn't done. Instead, we had government by acronym. According to the New Orleans emergency plan, "The Office of Emergency Preparedness (OEP) will coordinate with the Louisiana Office of Emergency Preparedness (LOEP)" and the Association of Contingency Planners (ACP). OEP and LOEP would conduct workshops at the Emergency Support Function (ESF) level to prepare Mass Casualty Incident (MCI) scenarios and learn Emergency Operating Center (EOC) procedure.

New Orleans planners also emphasized classwork: officials were to take LOEP courses and attend state hurricane conferences and workshops and the National Hurricane Conference (NHC). The city plan detailed specific ways for New Orleans to avoid chaos: for example, it unrealistically stipulated that two traffic control officers would be placed at each key intersection. The state plan stipulated that relief agencies were not to bring food and supplies into New Orleans because that would only slow down the evacuation.

The city plan also emphasized preparation through use of MCI scenarios and then more preparation: the OEP administrative and training officer would work with the LOEP state training officer to conduct workshops at the ESF level and to review EOC/ESF standard operating procedures. OEP officials attended "intensive work sessions with elements of the emergency response organizations in order to enhance unified disaster planning."

Perhaps New Orleans could have used even more planning and more meetings to unify the FEMA, OEP, LOEP, NHC, MCI, and ESF plans and experience. In any event, the plans were all on paper on Friday, August 26, when Governor Kathleen Babineaux Blanco examined the weather forecasts and declared a state of emergency for all of Louisiana, as did President Bush when he directed the Department of Homeland Security (DHS), and FEMA specifically, to coordinate disaster relief efforts.

BREAKDOWN: THE BEGINNING

City planning went into effect on Saturday, August 27, when Mayor Ray Nagin at a press conference offered two pieces of advice to his constituents: leave the city if you can, but if you have "special needs" use the Superdome as a "last resort," bringing with you "small quantities of food for three or four days, to be safe." Police superintendent Edward Compass also had his plan: he announced that looters would be "dealt with severely and harshly and prosecuted to the fullest extent of the law." But his plan did not take into account the hundreds of police who would go AWOL, or even join the looters.

At least 80 percent of New Orleans residents escaped in their cars, enduring long delays on the road but eventually getting away. Thousands who remained went to twelve locations and boarded Regional Transportation Authority buses that took them to the Superdome or other shelters within the city. By Sunday evening twenty-six thousand people were living in the Superdome, including six hundred with medical needs. Most had not brought food and water with them as requested, but all was not lost: the Louisiana National Guard made things more tolerable by delivering on Sunday evening ten truckloads of enough food and water to supply fifteen thousand people for three days.

Katrina struck New Orleans at 8:00 a.m. on Monday with an eighteen-foot storm surge and 120 mph winds. FEMA director Michael Brown arrived at the LOEP in Baton Rouge at 11:00 a.m. and said that the evacuation had gone according to plan: his words were, "very smooth." In the afternoon he sent DHS secretary Michael Chertoff a request for one thousand FEMA employees to report in two days to help in a variety of ways, particularly by helping residents fill out disaster relief forms. Paper ruled.

On Monday afternoon, as President Bush declared the states of Louisiana and Mississippi "major disaster areas," New Orleans officials expressed relief that Katrina had moved east and not given New Orleans a direct wallop. But during the afternoon a levee break at Seventeenth Street was flooding one-fifth of the city, and looters were carrying away clothes and shoes without opposition from Coleman's Retail Store at 4001 Earhart Boulevard.

As the waters rose, President Bush sent a message to New Orleans via a speech in Arizona: "The federal government has got assets and resources that we'll be deploying to help you." Shortly thereafter Michael Brown acknowledged that he was unable to get a team into downtown New

Orleans and thus could not give an estimate of what help would be needed. Then levees broke in seven places, and reports of grave danger rose with the water. Mayor Ray Nagin responded by emphasizing paperwork, telling reporters, "We're giving [FEMA] a hell of a list" of city needs.

By Tuesday much of New Orleans was underwater, and paper boats did not suffice. The city's Convention Center became one of the Shelters of Last Resort noted in the city plan, but since it was not listed by name in the planning documents that FEMA and Louisiana officials had, its use apparently came as a surprise to them. Soon more than twenty thousand people were in and around the center; yet as late as Thursday morning, on a National Public Radio interview, the DHS's Chertoff said he did not know that the Convention Center was being used.

Some people looted stores that sold computers, jewelry, and other goods, and at times police joined in. One of New Orleans's finest was immortalized on film as he loaded a shopping cart with a computer and a 27-inch flatscreen television. The Convention Center had little food or water and no police or national guardsmen on hand. Most of the city was calm, though, roiled largely by rumors of shootings and not the real thing.

MIDWEEK MORASS

Mayor Nagin visited the Convention Center on Wednesday, August 31, and reported that people "were panicked." He also seemed panicked and determined to justify his inaction by exaggerating the degree of havoc: "After the shootings and the looting got out of control, I did not go back in there. My security people advised me not to go back." Meanwhile, security people were telling residents looking for food or shelter to go to the Convention Center.

On Wednesday the Superdome was a hot, smelly, miserable place with broken toilets and low supplies of food and water, but (rumors to the contrary) no murders occurred there. Governor Blanco followed her plan that day by calling for Dome evacuation, but she still apparently did not know about the misery at the Convention Center. One reason she and many lesser officials showed confusion was that communication had faltered, with neither cell phones nor landlines operating. The fog of disaster is as dense as the fog of war.

The blame game quickly commenced. At the end of the week, Kenya Smith, head of intergovernmental relations for New Orleans, asserted that the city had never designated the Convention Center as an "official" shelter, and technically he was correct: he blamed hotels for sending guests there. He said that someone at the Convention Center told those arriving that FEMA would send buses to take them from the city, but federal officials apparently did not know a crowd was there until Thursday.

How great was the confusion? The *New Orleans Times-Picayune* had first started noticing the Convention Center's huddled masses on Wednesday, but (according to a LexisNexis search) network news shows did not start covering the mess there until Thursday. NBC initially presented a low-key report from a photographer, Tony Sambato, who had been in the building: "These are the families who listened to the authorities, who followed direction, who believed in the government. They were told to go to the Convention Center. They did. . . . They've been behaving. They have not started any melees, any riots, nothing. They just want food and support. There's no hostility there, so they don't need to be bringing any guns or anything like that. They need support."

On Thursday evening FEMA director Brown appeared befuddled but honest about his befuddlement: he told Ted Koppel on ABC's *Nightline* that he had only recently learned about the Convention Center refugees, and Koppel responded, "Don't you guys watch television? Our reporters have been reporting about it for more than just today." Not according to the LexisNexis records, though, which show the first ABC news show mention of the Convention Center on *World News Tonight* at 6:30 p.m. on Thursday.

The blame game included frequent outbursts about lack of planning, but as we've seen, plans existed in abundance and they transported as many people to safety as paper airplanes do. Governmental plans sometimes made things worse: the American Red Cross was ready to go to the Superdome on Monday or Tuesday to provide relief for the twenty-five thousand there, but the Louisiana Department of Homeland Security said such action ran counter to its plan, since a Red Cross presence "would keep people from evacuating and encourage others to come into the city."

Each group of officials—city, state, and federal—seemed to consider its plan preeminent, and each blamed others for not recognizing the true best of show. Mayor Nagin said, "Our plan never assumed people being in the Dome more than two or three days." City officials, anticipating that the city water system would fail, included in their plan the expectation that the National Guard would bring portable toilets to the Superdome. They never did.

PAPER JUNGLE

It soon became apparent that fears of litigation pushed many officials to submit to rule by paperocracy:

- On Sunday afternoon New Mexico governor Bill Richardson offered help from his state's National Guard and Governor Blanco accepted, but nothing happened because Washington did not get the paperwork done until Thursday.

- Twenty deputies and six emergency medical technicians from Loudon County, Virginia, were kept from helping because neither FEMA nor Louisiana authorities had acted on an emergency request from Jefferson Parish.

- Air Force Reserve Col. Tim Tarchick told CBS that his unit "could have been airborne in six hours and overhead plucking out people . . . but between all the agencies that have a part in the approval process it took thirty-four hours to get three of my helicopters airborne."

- Officials told the American Ambulance Association, which was ready to send three hundred emergency vehicles from Florida to the disaster area, that the General Services Administration needed to issue authorization. GSA said that FEMA had to do it. The ambulances never came.

- International helpers also were exasperated. It took four days for FEMA to give permission to Sweden to send a transport plane with a water purification system. U.S. officials slowed the arrival of Canadian search and rescue helicopters and ships, and took a week to say yes to a telecommunications company from the Netherlands.

Representative Bobby Jindal (R-LA) was one of many to complain about the bureaucratic problems that his constituents faced: "A mayor in my district tried to get supplies for his constituents, who were hit directly by the hurricane. He called for help and was put on hold for forty-five minutes. Eventually, a bureaucrat promised to write a memo to his supervisor. A sheriff in my district office reported being told that he would not get the resources his office needed to do its job unless he e-mailed a request. The parish was flooded and without electricity! My office became so frustrated with the bureaucracy that we often turned to private companies. They responded more quickly and flexibly."

Many doctors and nurses tried to volunteer through the National Disaster Medical System, but NDMS team leader Timothy Crowley, a doctor on the Harvard Medical School faculty, called the deployment a "total failure." He reported that his team was summoned late and was then left isolated in Baton Rouge for a week while New Orleans suffered. Finally, the team made it to the disaster zone and saw overwhelming needs. Crowley asked for reinforcements but was told that no help was available; he later found that many other teams were "sitting on their butts for days waiting and asking for missions." He concluded that the NDMS was "completely dysfunctional. I never learned what sort of political agenda or just plain incompetence or stupidity were behind these decisions."

ABC's John Stossel reported another aspect of paperocracy crippling health care: "Dr. Jeffrey Guy, a Nashville trauma surgeon, recruited four hundred doctors, nurses, and first responders to help the people in New Orleans. Then FEMA gave them something to do: fill out sixty-page applications that demanded photographs and tax forms."

Guy and his associates submitted, but the bureaucratic saga had just begun: he "received an e-mail from an emergency room doctor in Mississippi who needed bandages, splints, medicine, and coloring books for children. Guy had them—he'd been collecting corporate donations—but FEMA said they needed two state permits to transport these items from Tennessee to Mississippi. The supplies were only sent when two guys showed up with a church van and volunteered to take them—as rogue responders without FEMA's permission."

The rogue responders went in, but more fearful souls were holding back for fear of liability. Mayor Nagin, for example, had issued a voluntary evacuation on Saturday, August 27, but held off ordering a mandatory one until the next day because he was concerned that the city could be held financially liable for closing hotels and other businesses.

WHEN LEVEES SEEMED UNIMPORTANT

Finances played a role in the mayor's thinking, and as the blame game escalated, so did complaints that insufficient federal appropriations caused the flooding. Political and media leaders often claimed they had always fought vigorously for more spending on levees, but the miracle of Internet document retrieval shows frequent falsification of history. The *New York Times*, for example, blamed the White House and Congress for shorting flood control needs, but an April 2005 *Times* editorial sneered at "a bill now before the Senate Committee on Environment and Public Works. The bill would shovel $17 billion at the Army Corps of Engineers for flood control and other water-related projects—this at a time when President Bush is asking for major cuts in Medicaid and other important domestic programs."

The Medicaid issue has many sides, but the *Times* editorial's implication was clear: flood control was not an important domestic program. Besides, the pork percentage in public works spending was often so high that even liberal newspapers normally favoring more government spending were digging their heels into the mud or saying that the money could be spent much better elsewhere. State officials seemed asleep: in March 2005

FEMA ordered Louisiana to repay $30 million in flood control grants it had misused.

The board of directors of the Orleans Levee District, which had a $40 million annual budget, nearly three hundred employees, and the responsibility for most of the city's flood control, diverted millions it had for levee improvement into nonlevee projects such as a Mardi Gras foundation. The board spent hours of meeting time discussing its lease with the *Belle of Orleans* floating casino, its management of the lakefront marina and commuter airport it owns, its plans to string fiber-optic cable through levees, and its plans to build a $280 million man-made island in Lake Pontchartrain. The *Wall Street Journal* reported that one brochure defined the triple work of the levee board: "We protect against hurricanes, floods and boredom."

Given the small likelihood of a disaster striking in any particular year, bored politicians often put off prevention expenditures in favor of immediate job preservers and vote producers. In New Orleans, many officials disregarded the need for change and pocketed loose change. Bill Nungesser, a former Levee Board chairman, described his reform attempts this way: "Every time I turned over a rock, there was something rotten. I used to tell people, 'If your children ever die in a hurricane, come shoot us, because we're responsible.' We throw away all sorts of money."

Much of the money, though, was not merely thrown away; it enriched those with sticky fingers. Lou Riegel, the agent in charge of the FBI's New Orleans office, has described Louisiana's public corruption as "epidemic, endemic, and entrenched. No branch of government is exempt." No exemptions: last year three top state officials at the LOEP were indicted for allegedly obstructing a probe into how federal money found its way to owners of flood-prone homes.

The bottom line is that the charge of insufficient spending may be accurate, but the charge of insufficient allocation is not. The money was there. That it was misused came as no surprise to those who regularly scrutinize government budgets. Even the *Washington Post* acknowledged in December 2005 that federal spending to create the Department of Homeland Security had probably hurt rather than helped New Orleans, because it had created new levels of bureaucracy.

BEYOND LEADERSHIP PROBLEMS

So was the problem lack of leadership? Many have argued that Katrina showed not only New Orleans's unique geographic vulnerability but also its below-sea-level politics. Mayor Nagin gained a place in Louisiana's crowded political hall of shame by jumping to conclusions, casting blame like confetti, and often losing touch with reality. On Wednesday of hurricane week he ordered 1,500 police to stop looting, but that was more than all the members of the 1,450-member police force, and one-sixth of them were AWOL. He kept giving unrealistic commands, and the next day he exploded: "I need reinforcements. I need troops, man. I need five hundred buses."

Nagin, in short, was like a general who misuses his resources, sees his troops desert, and then asks for more of both. Nor was the mayor alone among local demagogues seemingly created in Huey Long's image. Aaron Broussard, president of Jefferson Parish, embellished a widely publicized story of a mother in a nursing home who supposedly begged her son for four days to rescue her from rising waters; the mother was dead before the flood came. New Orleans police chief Eddie Compass, who resigned after Katrina's chaos subsided, trumpeted false stories of child rape at the Superdome.

State officials also messed up. Nagin was wrong in his blame shifting but accurate in his facts when he said (on CNN on September 5) that Governor Blanco had turned down President Bush's initial offer to nationalize the relief effort when she met with him aboard Air Force One: the mayor said the governor asked for twenty-four hours to "think about it." She fiddled while Katrina approached. She also made a bad situation worse by not allowing the Red Cross to bring to the Superdome water, food, and blankets that it had prepositioned for emergency situations. State officials did not allow delivery because they did not want to attract more people to those sites.

And after a barrage of bad press on Wednesday, August 31, President Bush the next day said that the federal government should pick up the entire tab for relief efforts. Trying and failing to match his predecessor's awesome performances as the nation's First Emoter, he tried to counter criticism by promising a Clinton-style spending spree. This was wrong and wasteful: "They are throwing money out, they are shoveling it out the door," said James Albertine, who, as past president of the American League of Lobbyists, knows giveaways when he sees them.

The leadership failure was general: despite (or because of) all the planning, the list of snafus stretched from New Orleans to Washington. Blogger Rick Moran, who developed a thorough time line of the Katrina disaster, concluded, "I am convinced that any commission or congressional investigation —if even slightly impartial—will find enough stupidity, incompetence, panic, blame shifting, lying, and bureaucratic ass covering to sate the appetite for name calling and blame assigning of even the most partisan among us."

But why should we think that if leaders were different the populace would be content? When so many are discontented with government under normal situations, why should we think that it could satisfy people in an emergency? The brutal fact is that big government tends toward big bureaucracy, which means elaborate paper flow but the tendency of one misplaced card to bring down the house. If Nagin had been a strong leader and had used the hundreds of buses that were available to transport vulnerable residents out of town before the hurricane hit, where would they have gone? With in-state shelters inadequate for the task, would the Astrodome and other refuges have opened their doors wide absent the video of desperation that emerged from New Orleans?

The political willingness to innovate is rarely present except in response to disaster. Democracies typically lurch from crisis to crisis, often fighting the last war and looking through the rearview mirror to see what's up ahead. That's bad, but the autocratic alternative is worse. We complain about government moving with the speed of a brontosaurus, but we also would not want it reacting like a raptor, tearing at the flesh of anything in its way.

But let's assume the improbable: maybe leadership will be much better the next time a disaster hits. Since a major American city hadn't faced a disaster of such magnitude since 9/11, and since New Orleans is uniquely vulnerable, maybe this was a learning experience for the entire country. Maybe next time things will work smoothly. Maybe.

And yet, the "maybe" we should most keep in mind is that next time things might be much worse. New Orleans could easily have been in even worse shape that it was during September. What if Katrina had not ticked right to come ashore just east of New Orleans and head over the swamplands into Mississippi, leaving the city on the western, less dangerous side of the hurricane? Had Katrina held its course and its full strength, it probably would have ripped most of the roof right off the Superdome—and the roof holds up the walls. Casualties there and elsewhere in the city could have been in the tens of thousands rather than the hundreds.

But there is a deeper question: How likely is it that government will save us even in the best of circumstances, let alone in those close to the worst?

Chapter 2

WHAT THE PRESS REPORTED

Many journalistic organizations were self-congratulatory at the end of the first week of Katrina misery. Reporters had apparently stood up for the oppressed and taken it to "the man." They had focused national attention on the trauma of those left behind at the Superdome and Convention Center.

The reality was different. National media had become a megaphone for hysteria and blame. Among the casualties were truth, speed in offering help, and progress in both international affairs and domestic race relations.

Let's first look at hysteria, much of it coming from local officials. In interviews with Oprah Winfrey and other journalists, Police Chief Compass spoke of "little babies getting raped." Mayor Nagin described "hundreds of armed gang members killing and raping people" inside the Dome and requested ten thousand body bags. *Editor & Publisher* headlined one of its stories "Mortuary Director Tells Local Paper 40,000 Could Be Lost in Hurricane."

What should have been dismissed as gossip quickly became media gospel. Reporters circulated rumors of hundreds of gang members killing people at the Superdome and "thirty or forty bodies" stored in a Convention Center freezer. (Actual number: zero.) Shelters purportedly featured shoot-outs while snipers supposedly fired at doctors and rescue helicopters from high-rises. Soldiers at night were purportedly racing toward muzzle flashes to disarm well-armed criminals. The *Los Angeles Times* reported "snipers and armed mobs" terrorizing "seething crowds of refugees." (Never happened.)

Other lowlights included CNN's Paula Zahn speaking of "bands of rapists, going block to block." (There were no such bands.) National Public Radio's John Burnett told listeners that a thirteen-year-old was reportedly raped and killed in a Convention Center bathroom. (No such death occurred, and the *New Orleans Times-Picayune* was unable to confirm any rapes there.) Fox News's Geraldo Rivera's novelistic sense was as good as ever when he spoke of how "the sun set on a scene of terror, chaos, confusion, anarchy, violence, rapes, murders, dead babies, dead people."

The nonjournalists were often worse. Oprah Winfrey told her fans that in the Superdome "gangs banded together and had more ammunition, at times, than the police." It was as if New Orleans streets had become the set for a reality show. At the extreme, some even went from excitement to incitement: on *Air America Radio*, Randi Rhodes repeatedly urged poor listeners in hurricane areas to loot away, avoiding discount centers and hitting the high-end stores. Newspapers abroad exaggerated further. The French newspaper *Liberation* cooked up a detailed story of twelve hundred people drowning at one school.

It was hard to top, though, the live report of CNN's Chris Lawrence, who stood on a tall building and babbled on about how "helicopters are literally just completely surrounding the city. . . . There have literally been groups of young men roaming the city, shooting at people, attempting to rape women. . . . We were at the New Orleans Convention Center today and saw mothers with their babies literally living in raw sewage. . . . People are literally dying at the Convention Center." That news show's anchor, Paula Zahn, then chimed in about "literally, people walking around in feces."

Those stories, at best metaphorical but largely mendacious, literally led to good ratings, and facts had a hard time catching up. Orleans Parish DA Eddie Jordan later said that four murders had occurred in the entire city during the week after Katrina hit, making it a typical week in a city that anticipates more than two hundred homicides per year. From the press, he said, "I had the impression that at least forty or fifty murders had occurred" at the Superdome and Convention Center alone. He said national media reporters heard rumors and did "nothing to follow up on any of these cases; they just accepted what people told them."

Inside the Superdome, where National Guard Troops performed rigorous security checks before allowing anyone inside, only one shooting was verified. That one, which injured Louisiana guardsman Chris Watt of the 527th Engineer Battalion, was widely misreported, according to Maj. David Baldwin, who led the team of soldiers that arrested the alleged assailant. Watt's attacker hit him with a metal rod, and Watt accidentally shot himself in the leg during the subsequent arrest of the assailant.

At the worst site, the Convention Center, massive looting occurred and some inside cowered in fear, but "everything was embellished, everything was exaggerated," said Deputy Police Superintendent Warren Riley. Jimmie Fore, vice president of the state authority that runs the center, stayed in the building with a core group of thirty-five employees until Thursday. He reported that thugs looted food and booze, but neither he nor any of his employees saw any violent crimes. The frozen corpses story apparently originated with some Arkansas National Guard members who heard the rumors in a food line and passed them on to reporters who amplified them. A formal Guard review of the matter later found that no soldier had seen the corpses.

Frontline law enforcement officers scorned the exaggerations put out by drive-by reports and desk-bound officials. Sgt. First Class Jason Lachney, a Superdome patroller, described press reports as "99 percent [expletive]. . . . Bad things happened, but I didn't see any killing and raping and cutting of throats or anything . . . 99 percent of the people in the Dome were very well-behaved." Dr. Louis Cataldie, the state Health and Human Services official who oversees body-recovery missions, bemoaned the false reports that flooded his staff. New Orleans coroner Frank Minyard said he had seen only seven gunshot victims during hurricane week: "Seven gunshots isn't even a good Saturday night in New Orleans."

Author Michael Lewis, who grew up in New Orleans, was one of the few who, instead of accepting gossip, did what reporters are supposed to do: he checked out the stories and noted, "So far as I can tell—and I covered much of the city, along with every inch of the high ground—very few of the many terrible things that people are reported to have done to one another ever happened." The police had said that gangs of young black men were looting and killing their way across the city. Lewis checked hundreds of houses and found that none had been broken into. He said, "The Ace Hardware store on Oak Street was supposed to have had its front wall pulled off by a forklift, but it appeared to be, like most stores and all houses, perfectly intact."

JOURNALISTIC SEMI-APOLOGIES

Later in September some journalists were defensive. NPR managing editor Bill Marimow explained its false reports by saying, "At the Convention Center, it was extremely dangerous . . . not the kind of place one would venture into and begin searching for dead bodies." Many editors talked about the lack of telephone service. But other stories emerged from celebrity journalists alighting only momentarily in New Orleans to light up their stories with a dateline of authenticity. Few spent hours in a hot arena or headed into neighborhoods along with grimy work crews. Instead of telling the stories of ordinary people who did extraordinary things, they tended to report only what *US News & World Report* emphasized on its cover: "WHAT WENT WRONG."

Only after the initial reporting had circled the globe did newspapers throughout the country, led by the *Times-Picayune*, admit some of their errors, acknowledging, "The vast majority of reported atrocities committed by evacuees at the Dome—murders, rapes and beatings—have turned out to be false." But by then the damage was done; press summaries after the spotlight was moved could not compensate for fervent broadcast stories and front-page headlines when the world was watching and groaning.

The *New York Times*, still viewed by some as the newspaper of record, sheepishly corrected part of the record a month after the fact, acknowledging on September 29 that "the most alarming stories that coursed through the city appear to be little more than figments of frightened imaginations." Some examples: a team of paramedics delayed entering one area "for nearly 10 hours based on a state trooper's report that a mob of armed, marauding people had commandeered boats. It turned out to be two men escaping from their flooded streets. . . . A contingent of National Guard troops was sent to rescue a St. Bernard Parish deputy sheriff who radioed for help, saying he was pinned down by a sniper. Accompanied by a SWAT team, the troops surrounded the area. The shots turned out to be the relief valve on a gas tank that popped open every few minutes."

Media exaggeration was not a victimless crime. Reporters pushed politicians to make grand promises of financial aid, but they also slowed down the arrival of responders who, based on press reports, had to plan missions as military and not just philanthropic endeavors. Commanders had to provide armed escorts for doctors and rescuers on any short trip, even crossing the street. Soldiers on hot days felt it necessary to don heavy body armor, which also slowed them down. New Orleans police stopped their search-and-rescue operations and turned their attention to the imagined mobs of rapists.

The same rumors of rampant Convention Center violence that scared NPR prompted Louisiana National Guard Col. Jacques Thibodeaux to put together a one-thousand man force of soldiers and police in full battle gear to secure the center at noon on Friday, September 2. His soldiers met no resistance and took control in twenty minutes. Thibodeaux said his forces found no murder, rape, assault evidence, witnesses, or victims. One FEMA physician who believed media reports arrived at the Superdome with a refrigerated 18-wheeler and three doctors to process bodies. He expected to cart away two hundred bodies but had to settle for six.

CNN's Sanjay Gupta reported that two patients died while waiting for evacuation helicopters that had been grounded for a day by the false reports of sniper fire. Gupta noted that "the inability to get people out of these hospitals is frightening." However, it was press scare tactics that caused the delay.

The head of the ambulance service evacuating the sick and injured from the Superdome suspended operations at one point. When told that the National Guard was sending one hundred military police to take control, he said, "We need a thousand."

THE POLITICAL ANGLE

Press hysteria interacted with Bush bashing and black stereotyping in a way likely to cause long-range damage to budgets and race relations.

Regarding the president, Keith Olbermann on MSNBC nominated "two words which will define his government, our government: New Orleans. For him, it is a shame, in all senses of the word." Howell Raines, formerly the *New York Times* executive editor, wrote in the *Los Angles Times*, "The populism of Huey Long was financially corrupt, but when it came to the welfare of people, it was caring. [Under] the churchgoing cultural populism of George Bush . . . the poor drown in their attics."

MSNBC's Chris Matthews and many others said that Katrina demonstrated the need for an even larger federal government. ABC reporter Chris Cuomo called Katrina "perhaps the most economically destructive event in American history since the Great Depression, the last time the country responded with unprecedented sweeping changes to help the least fortunate. Today may demand an equal effort." Eleanor Clift on *Newsweek*'s Web site also saw the silver lining: "If there's an upside to Katrina, it's that the Republican agenda of tax cuts, Social Security privatization and slashing government programs is over."

Reporters retailed blame for not doing enough planning or spending enough money, and the leading screamers received praise. *USA Today* headlined one story "Katrina Rekindles Adversarial Media," and the *New York Times* praised the way "normally poised, placid TV reporters now openly deplore the government's failure to help the victims adequately." ABC's Diane Sawyer, Charles Gibson, Ted Koppel, and George Stephanopoulos all pushed for higher taxes to pay for New Orleans reconstruction, as did NPR's Nina Totenberg.

The mission to force on-camera promises of more government spending was triumphant, initially. As Jason DeParle reported in the *New York Times*, Katrina excited liberals: "The issues they most cared about—health care, housing, jobs, race—were suddenly staples of the news." But as word spread about false reporting, the glitter disappeared, and DeParle reported on October 11 that "what looked like a chance to talk up new programs is fast becoming a scramble to save the old ones."

"We've had a stunning reversal in just a few weeks," complained Robert Greenstein, director of the Center on Budget and Policy Priorities, a liberal advocacy group in Washington. But whose fault was it? Propaganda about German atrocities in Belgium fueled sentiment for the United States to become involved in World War I. When the truth came out, Americans felt bamboozled and moved toward isolationism, which allowed for the rise of Hitler. British and French populaces also distrusted what seemed in the 1930s to be more scare stories about the Germans: the larger effect of World War I propaganda may have been to bring about World War II.

With Katrina it soon became apparent that some of the promises made in passion probably would not be kept, with one result being a new chapter in the "Bush lies" book. Meanwhile the international image of America, crucial to the war on terror, took a big hit: Sajeewa Chinthaka of Sri Lanka was typical of viewers abroad who received one side of the news and said, "I am absolutely disgusted. After the tsunami our people, even the ones who lost everything, wanted to help the others who were suffering." That's exactly what happened in New Orleans, but it was rarely reported.

Instead, make-believe shots were heard around the world. *Agence France-Presse* triumphantly told the story of "gunbattles and fistfights in the southern jazz capital . . . with some gunned down outside the local convention center." An Australian report claimed, "Rescuers and police were shot at as New Orleans descended into anarchy today. . . . Police chief Eddie Compass said he sent in 88 officers to quell the situation at the Superdome, but they were quickly beaten back by an angry mob." None of that happened.

Similarly, the *Daily Mail* in London declared, "Law and order is gone, gunmen roam at will, raping and looting, and as people die of heat and thirst, bodies lie rotting in the street. Until now, such a hellish vista could only be imagined in a Third World disaster zone. But this was America yesterday."

No, it wasn't. *Folha* of Brazil reported rampant death in the Superdome, "a stadium of seventy-five floors." This last statement is remarkable, since with that number of floors, the 273-foot-high dome could have at its tallest point ceilings only 3.64 feet high.

LIBERAL RACISM

The future of race relations took an even bigger hit, once liberal press entrepreneurs framed the story as one of rich people not caring about poor people or whites not caring about blacks, and President Bush and his associates not caring about anyone other than their cronies. Some angry New Orleans residents at a congressional hearing in December 2005 charged that racism caused delays in Hurricane Katrina relief and rescue. They were right, but they misidentified the culprit. One reason for the delays was that some politicians and journalists painted a portrait of impoverished, over-whelmingly African-American masses of flood victims resorting to utter depravity, randomly attacking each other as well as the police and rescue workers trying to protect and save them. In Mayor Nagin's words, many of his constituents were in an "almost animalistic state."

Four days after the storm hit, black political organizer Randall Robinson said the "thousands of blacks in New Orleans . . . have begun eating corpses to survive." Even for those who see cannibalism as benign, a feast after only four days is premature. CNN became hysterical about "groups of young men roaming the city, shooting at people, attempting to rape women." None of this was true, and *New Orleans Times-Picayune* editor Jim Maoss also noted, after the fact, that if media had been characterizing the attitudes of "sweaty, hungry, desperate, white people, middle-class white people, it's hard to believe that these kinds of myths would have sprung up quite as readily."

Maoss referred to the reports of residents shooting at rescue helicopters as "classic urban myth." He noted that one report "was the result of a truck rolling over a sealed plastic bottle and producing an explosive sound, and everybody was predisposed to believe that, that it had to be gunshot." Coast Guard Lt. Chris Huberty, who flew one of those rescue helicopters purportedly under fire, also resented negative press characterizations of black New Orleans residents: "There were plenty of people sacrificing for others, regardless of their demographic."

When Wolf Blitzer on CNN at the end of the week said, "Had this happened in a predominantly white community, the federal government would have responded much more quickly," he was probably right. Had not reporters made racist assumptions about black behavior, rescuers would not have had to view their operations as demanding military precaution rather than humanitarian speed. Had commanders not seen the need to arrive at the Convention Center with overwhelming force, they would have been able to evacuate people from there a day earlier.

Instead of tamping down hysteria, network talkers regularly stirred up racial anger. On NBC, anchor Brian Williams lectured that the hurricane would "necessitate a national discussion on race, oil, politics, class, infrastructure, the environment, and more." On ABC, Ted Koppel began by orating that New Orleans is 67 percent black, and "the slow response to the victims of Hurricane Katrina has led to questions about race, poverty, and a seemingly indifferent government." CNN's Blitzer referred to hurricane victims as "so poor and so black," and prodded interviewees to find racism in the government's response.

The result of network ignorance and bias, as Michael Lewis observed, was that some people during Katrina week had an "informational disadvantage": working TV sets. Over and over and over again, they replayed the same few horrifying scenes from the Superdome, the Convention Center, and a shop in downtown New Orleans. If the images were to be reduced to a sentence in the minds of Uptown New Orleans, that sentence would be: "Crazy black people with automatic weapons are out hunting white people, and there's no bag limit."

Mainstream journalists, of course, pleaded innocent to incitement and said that they were merely showing what Katrina has shown: that blacks were second-class citizens. *CBS Sunday Morning* commentator Nancy Giles was typical in declaring that if most of those who remained in New Orleans had been white, "they would not have gone for days without food and water. . . . They would have been rescued and relocated a hell of a lot faster."

As chapter 1 pointed out, they wouldn't have been rescued faster under any of the standard plans. Singer Kanye West talked about how George Bush doesn't care about black people: "They have been trying to sweep us under the kitchen sink." Oprah megaphoned Nagin's charge: "If this thing were to happen in Miami, in LA, or Chicago, we would have had everything we need." But significant help came sooner after Katrina than after Hurricane Andrew hit Florida in 2002—in spots where military security was not seen as essential, in three days rather than five.

The facts of death also suggest that Katrina was an equal opportunity drowner. Of the identified victims released to families from a makeshift morgue in St. Gabriel, 44 percent were African-American, 47 percent Caucasian, 3 percent Hispanic, and 8 percent unknown. Nor were blacks the only ones to see their homes destroyed; in 95 percent white St. Bernard Parish, Katrina's storm surge demolished 95 percent of homes. One broadcaster from that parish noted: "It was over five days before the Federal Government showed up. . . . Sixty-six thousand people live in my parish. . . . They're picking up pets in the city, and I still have people in the attics trapped, waiting on roofs for someone to come rescue them."

At the end of 2005, Knight-Ridder reported: "Four months after Hurricane Katrina, analyses of data suggest that some widely reported assumptions about the storm's victims were incorrect. . . . The victims weren't disproportionately poor. . . . They also weren't disproportionately African American." Knight-Ridder reported that the elderly were the major victims: "People sixty and older account for only about 15 percent of the population in the New Orleans area, but the Knight-Ridder database found that 74 percent of the dead were sixty or older. Nearly half were older than seventy-five. Lack of transportation was assumed to be a key reason that many people stayed behind and died, but at many addresses where the dead were found, their cars remained in their driveways, flood-ruined symbols of fatal miscalculation."

Once the hysteria washed away and a backlash against hurricane hyperbole emerged, both officials and journalists tried to explain why they had gotten the story wrong. Nagin and Compass said that they were relaying stories that they thought to be true at the time, but that they also wanted to spark a national reaction. Reporters said that they were following standard procedure by interviewing official sources. Many journalists let empathy for those left behind trample standard skepticism; this easily forgivable lapse affected reporters of all perspectives. Television reporters could not resist emotional drama; network stars also wanted to display what passed as compassion.

Then mainstream media liberalism kicked in almost automatically: reporters not only served as lapdogs for purposeful or ignorant exaggerations by local officials but also quickly added hype of their own. Since few reporters knew what was happening, and a pack journalism atmosphere developed wherever reporters congregated in places of safety, the constraints of competition that sometimes staunch flows of bathos were not present. Besides, crying and yelling made for much better ratings than calm assessment of the damages.

Chapter 3

DÉJÀ VU, 1950–2004

ow that we've examined government and media failure concerning Katrina, let's put this in context by examining how we arrived at this point.

One initial lesson is clear: America is an exceptional country, but it is not exempt from the need to expect the unexpected. An earthquake shook Bostonians in 1755. A hurricane in 1781 prevented British reinforcements from making it to Yorktown in support of General Cornwallis. Three earthquakes centered at New Madrid, Missouri, in 1811 and 1812 probably measured over 8.0 on the Richter scale. (These earthquakes did little damage to humans, but a similarly powerful earthquake today would ravage St. Louis and other large cities.) A fire burned Chicago in 1871, and "grasshopper ravages" tortured Great Plains settlers. A dam break and flood destroyed Johnstown, Pennsylvania, in 1889. A hurricane smashed Galveston, Texas, in 1900. And so it goes.

In every case relief for the victims began immediately, with civic and fraternal organizations, churches, and other nongovernmental groups often taking the lead role. The federal government did not overlook damage: Congress often passed declarations expressing sympathy but maintained that businesses or charitable groups were best suited to act expeditiously and with discernment. And so they did: the Chicago Aid and Relief Society, which coordinated assistance for two years after the great fire of 1871, met immediate needs for food and clothing but did not create long-term dependency. While the government concentrated on keeping order, the society provided help in restarting businesses, reopening stores and medical offices, and providing sewing machines so that victims could get back to work quickly and help themselves.

The 1880s witnessed the advent of the American Red Cross, formed in 1881. During the decade it sent supplies to victims of a forest fire near Port Huron, Michigan, and to Pennsylvania survivors of the Johnstown flood in 1889. The Red Cross also helped the largely African-American victims of a hurricane that hit Sea Island, Georgia, in 1893. In all these instances, Red Cross representatives arriving at a stricken community found an ad hoc local or regional relief committee already collecting and distributing relief funds and supplies.

One other 1880s disaster led to a breakdown of congressional restraint. When West Texas in 1886 and 1887 faced an enormous drought, Congress passed a bill appropriating $10,000 for the distribution of seeds to farmers in the area. President Grover Cleveland, though, vetoed the bill, arguing that it was wrong "to indulge a benevolent and charitable sentiment through the appropriation of funds for that purpose." He expressed a hope that private and church philanthropy would come through.

The press response to Cleveland's veto was astounding: the *Dallas Morning News* supported it, even though the appropriation would have benefited some of its own readers. The *News* also editorialized that Cleveland's veto message "recalled Congress more strictly to constitutional lines of thought" and at the same time "advertised in a special manner to the whole country the deplorable fact of the suffering." The *Morning News* established a relief fund and asked for contributions, as did the *Louisville Courier-Journal*, which proclaimed, "We believe Kentucky alone will send $10,000 in seed or in money. She will . . . justify the President's confidence that the people will do what is right."

Other journalists emphasized the words of American Red Cross founder Clara Barton after she toured the troubled area: "The counties which have suffered from drought need help, without doubt, but not help from Congress." Contributions soon arrived from Texas, Kentucky, and other states. West Texas eventually received not $10,000 of federal funds but over $100,000 in private aid.

Some events came suddenly: in March 1888 three to four feet of snow fell from Maryland to Maine in what became known as the Great White Hurricane, with winds of up to 48 mph creating snowdrifts up to fifty feet high. Two hundred ships were grounded and probably eighteen hundred people died. Sometimes individuals and companies took precautions to reduce their risk from storms. The owners of the endangered Brighton Beach Hotel at New York's Coney Island in 1888 jacked up the structure and used flatcars to move it 450 feet inland.

Even disasters that took an enormous total in lives did not lead to federal sustenance. The hurricane that killed over six thousand people in Galveston, Texas, in 1900 motivated an elderly Clara Barton to set up shop there for several months—once again relief was nongovernmental. The rebuilding process commenced with Galveston County, not the federal government, beginning work on what became a sixteen-foot-high seawall that extended for six miles. Washington did pay for an extension to protect federal military land.

DEBATES ABOUT FEDERAL INVOLVEMENT

San Francisco rebounded from its 1906 earthquake (probably a 7.8 on the Richter scale) with help from the Red Cross—which President Theodore Roosevelt officially designated as the lead relief agency—and with money from insurance payments (downtown business buildings had been well insured). Since the devastating postearthquake fires owed their spread to an inadequate city water supply, local authorities in San Francisco acted boldly. With state and federal agreement, and over the objections of famed protoenvironmentalist John Muir, they damned Yosemite National Park's Hetch Hetchy River and built a 150-mile aqueduct to flow water to the city.

The federal government issued no appropriations for disaster relief after a hurricane struck Miami in 1926 and caused over $40 billion in damage in today's dollars, or after the Mississippi River flood in 1927 covered twenty-seven thousand square miles. Nongovernmental relief efforts, though, were large: in 1927 the Red Cross cared for 325,000 flood evacuees in its own camps and fed 311,000 more in private homes. The first hurricane-related congressional appropriation came in 1928 as a demonstration of concern for an impoverished U.S. territory, with $8.1 million going to Puerto Ricans, largely for purchasing seeds and rebuilding schoolhouses. That same year Congress did not act in response to a hurricane that blew across Lake Okeechobee in Florida and sent a wall of water through lakeside towns, killing over one thousand.

Still, with the Puerto Rico precedent in place, officials began arguing that disaster relief in the forty-eight states should be a federal responsibility as well. Congress debated these questions in 1935 after a category 5 hurricane hit the Florida Keys on Labor Day, killing 259 veterans who were employed to build the southernmost section of U.S. 1 as part of a New Deal highway project, along with 164 civilians.

The vets were there because Franklin Roosevelt did not want to repeat the Hoover administration's politically disastrous decision to have U.S. troops (commanded by Douglas MacArthur) forcibly destroy a Washington encampment of jobless veterans demanding Depression help. When some vets reassembled in Washington after FDR's inauguration, he dispatched them to the Keys, where they were paid $30 a month plus food, housed in three beachfront work camps, and told to show the world the effectiveness of New Deal relief efforts. But when the hurricane approached, camp supervisors waited too long to order an evacuation by rail: 200 mph winds and an eighteen-foot storm surge tossed aside the train before the vets could climb aboard.

Federal officials and public relations specialists quickly headed to Florida, as conspiracy buffs complained about the "Veterans Extermination Bureau" in Washington, D.C., and the *Miami Herald* speculated that the disaster "may become a vital issue in next year's presidential election." Ernest Hemingway wrote for the Marxist magazine *New Masses* a furious article, "Who Killed the Vets?" Roosevelt's designee in Florida said the deaths were due to "an act of God," but the Miami Ministerial Association protested that designation. An investigation by the Veterans Administration, still full of Republican appointees, later concluded that federal officials were at fault, but the Roosevelt-backing *Washington Post* and *New York Times* ignored that report. Meanwhile, Florida governor David Sholtz flew from Tallahassee to Miami and took charge of the relief effort, still not seen as a federal responsibility.

The following year Republicans introduced a bill to compensate the families of the vets who died, since they were working on a federal project and were dead because of misfeasance by federal employees. John Rankin, a Mississippi Democrat who was on FDR's reelection team and chaired the House Committee on World War Veterans' Legislation, conducted hearings that skillfully obscured major evidence. Congress ended up approving small payments to vets' families because, as Wisconsin Representative Harry Sauthoff put it, "It must be remembered that the government put them there. The government had a responsibility and a duty."

In other circumstances, though, Washington had no responsibility. When the Ohio River flooded in 1936, covering half of Louisville and nearly all of Paducah, Kentucky, and Cairo, Illinois, 1.5 million endangered persons in twelve states left their homes. The Red Cross temporarily housed about half of the evacuees—using schools, church buildings, auditoriums, and tent cities—and extended some form of aid to many of the rest, but not with taxpayer dollars.

And yet federal disaster policy grew incoherent as the New Deal philosophy of relief set in: if the federal government took charge in times of economic depression, why not in emergency situations? When a hurricane struck New England in 1938, Congress allocated $5 million toward forest rehabilitation. The next decade brought more adhocracy, so when

Minnesota suffered flooding in 1950 and Rep. Harold Hagen asked his colleagues to provide relief for his state, he introduced a Disaster Relief Act designed merely to create "an orderly and continuing method of rendering assistance to the states and local governments in alleviating suffering and damage."

During brief floor debate, Rep. Edward Cox (D-GA) also said the bill was no big deal: "It simply establishes a fund to enable the government to give direct relief to these disaster areas when disasters arise, rather than having to come to Congress in each instance." The bill's price tag, only $5 million, was deliberately small. Some in the Senate suspected that the effort would grow. Virginia's Absalom Willis Robertson (the father of Pat Robertson) asked the bill's floor manager, John McClelland, to define the size of a covered disaster, but Senator McClelland refused the bait, saying merely that in every case it would be the president's decision, and "we can certainly rely upon whomever may be the President of the United States having some judgment and also some humanitarian feelings in making a decision as to what is a major disaster, where people have suffered."

The legislators may have believed that local and state officials would call upon federal help only in dire emergency, because any transfer of funds or material demanded a declaration by the president that an affected locality and state could not take care of business on its own. The supposition was that few mayors or governors would want to plead helplessness, and in those days that was probably true: local and state officials often acted proudly independent. The legislation stipulated that federal aid was only for "supplementing" efforts by those closest to the scene and would never replace them.

Another supposed check on the growth of federal disaster spending was the stipulation that local or state governments could borrow federal resources but would not be given them, and that food or medicine would be provided not by the government but by the Red Cross. Federal funds could also be used to make "emergency repairs to and temporary replacement of public facilities of local governments," but legislators banned use of funds for permanent replacement.

EXPANDING THE FEDERAL ROLE

Disaster relief, like Social Security and Medicaid, started quietly but soon grew, in part because thirteen times through 1980 Congress responded to other disasters by slowly expanding the scope of federal aid. The first change came only one year after passage of the initial relief act: following the 1951 Midwest flood, Missouri native Harry Truman pushed successfully for a Disaster Relief Act that provided funds for housing for victims. A 1953 tornado in Worcester, Massachusetts, brought congressional permission to give away federal surplus property for a good cause. In 1956 Congress agreed to pay most of the cost of replenishing beaches after storms swept away sand.

So it went. Each subsequent disaster led to new benefits, often added one by one, including unemployment compensation and grants for temporary housing, legal help, and mental health. Cities became eligible for funding to offset lost tax revenues, and soon permanent rather than temporary replacement of buildings was allowed. As one scholar, Mary Comerio, concluded, "Every few years, a new disaster demonstrated a particular local need. That need would be met with a new program or special funds. Each time, the programs would be carried forward to the next event."

Year by year the checks on spending diminished. In the beginning the federal government was merely supposed to add a little to what cities and states spent, but from the early 1950s through the mid-1970s, the federal share of disaster costs rose from 1 to 70 percent. One last stand against huge spending was that city and state governments would have to put in at least one dollar for every three dollars the federal government spent in a crisis, but after a while the president received authority to reduce or eliminate that percentage if he deemed that wise. Over time, cities and states could even pay their small share of the overall amount by using money from federal sources. Following the Midwest flood of 1993, for example, nonfederal entities paid their part of the disaster costs by using Community Development Block Grant funds that Washington had previously bestowed upon them.

Year by year politicians' responses to disasters extended the types of difficulties covered under federal legislation. The list in the 1950 law included flood, drought, fire, hurricane, earthquake, or storm. Subsequently, Congress told federal officials to react to tornadoes, high water (not just floods), wind-driven water (not just floods), tidal wave, tsunami, volcanic eruption, landslide, mudslide, snowstorm, and explosion.

Soon officials began to see that some federal payments following floods could be counterproductive. After Hurricane Betsy struck in 1965, the Task Force on Federal Flood Control Policy formed by the Bureau of the Budget cautioned that federal payments "could exacerbate the whole problem of flood losses" if they were offered to owners involved in "rebuilding destroyed or obsolete structures on the flood plain." Money given to those rebuilding on the same spot "would aggravate flood damages and constitute gross public irresponsibility."

Politics and philosophy overcame such caution: a Great Society, by definition, was one that would not accept defeat by hurricanes and floods! In 1966 President Lyndon Johnson transmitted the flood control task force report to Congress but also issued Executive Order 11926, which emphasized the need to deal with the "toll in personal hardship" and suggested the need for more "state and local regulation of use of lands exposed to flood hazard."

This order set the pattern for the next four decades. Local officials were supposed to stare down developers and refuse to give permits for building in areas likely to flood, even though that would constrain their tax base. Federal rules also stipulated that if developers gained permission, Washington would still sell low-cost flood insurance to those who built unwisely, or would even pay off uninsured owners if the disaster was sufficiently dramatic. The message was clear: don't play with matches, but if you do play with them and burn down your house, Uncle Sam is likely to pay you to build a new one.

This teaching troubled from the start some observers of housing and human nature, such as Housing and Urban Development undersecretary Robert C. Wood, who testified before Congress in 1967, "It would not be logical as a matter of public policy to permit insurance to be made available in localities which did not . . . assure that their citizens would not unknowingly acquire and develop property where it is subject to known flood hazards."

"Gross public irresponsibility . . . it would not be logical"—strong words that would be ignored. Perhaps that was inevitable, given the Great Society politics of the 1960s. Optimism about government pervaded the Kennedy and Johnson administrations, so it was logical to see Washington officials as those who would make plans both to reduce the scope of disaster and to pay off those who nevertheless became victims. The small-government view of construction in areas likely to flood, burn, or be shattered by earthquake was: you may build there legally, but insurance will be expensive; and if you go without, you will most likely lose all you have, so think twice before building there. That perspective was a political nonstarter.

And so the federal role in disaster relief grew, despite concerns about the growing counterproductivity of much expenditure. The 1965 Southeast Hurricane Disaster Relief Act led to the 1968 National Flood Insurance Act. These then led to the 1970 Federal Disaster Relief Act, which President Richard Nixon requested to address "gaps and overlaps" resulting from "fifty separate congressional enactments and executive actions." But this act merely created more gaps and overlaps. Following the 1971 San Fernando earthquake, federal officials were allowed to forgive up to $2,500 in loans. The *Los Angeles Times* found that funds were used for purposes not related to earthquake damages, with many applicants learning about the maximum allowed and filling out forms so as to get that amount..

In 1973 a White House policy document argued that federal disaster assistance was replacing rather than supplementing other efforts: "Benefits were so generous that individuals, businesses, and communities had little incentive to take initiatives to reduce personal and local hazards." Nevertheless, the 1974 Federal Disaster Relief Act once again expanded Washington's role by making occurrences classified not as "major disasters" but as "emergencies" eligible for aid.

The distinction was not clear, but presidents now had more flexibility, since they were also authorized to make "fire management assistance declarations." With governors being the ones to make catastrophe requests, presidents had a clear opportunity to reward friends and punish opponents; presidents from the 1950s through the 1980s (none acting like

Grover Cleveland) approved about 67 percent of declaration requests. The 1974 act also made the federal government liable for additional disaster-caused damages, such as those to a private nonprofit facility.

Jimmy Carter, trying to make sense of disaster relief, established FEMA by executive order in 1979, stating that the new structure will "permit more rational decisions of the relative costs and benefits of alternative approaches to disasters." That year Hurricane Frederic pummeled the Gulf Coast, leading analysts to estimate that it would be cheaper for the federal government to buy undeveloped coastal barriers than to subsidize their development and then rebuilding. That year also, the Unified National Program for Floodplain Management declared that cities and states should have effective "floodplain management programs . . . as a prerequisite to federal expenditures for the modification of flooding or of the impacts of flooding."

ATTEMPTS AT REFORM

Organizational changes and fervid declarations were on paper. In practice nothing significantly changed, however, even though the U.N. labeled the 1980s the International Decade for Natural Disaster Reduction and the Reagan administration tried to do its part domestically. The General Accounting Office in 1981 analyzed thirty-one requests from governors and found a "lack of consistency in the quality and method of assessments . . . [that] creates doubt as to whether the federal government is only providing supplementary assistance and whether each request is judged in a fair and equitable manner."

Under Reagan, FEMA drafted regulations that attempted to cut federal disaster expenditures by stiffening the criteria for declaring disaster and reducing Washington's share of disaster costs from 75 to 50 percent. One outside analyst, Bruce B. Clary, observed in 1985 that disaster assistance often "promoted poor locational decisions, since the federal government was subsidizing much of the risk." But opposition from congresspeople and local government officials killed the FEMA proposal in 1986. The substitute for action that year was another Unified National Program for Floodplain

Management that declared development in floodplains "should be avoided unless it is considered necessary from a public interest standpoint." Cities, of course, had a public interest in increasing their tax base.

A bill that became the Coastal Barrier Resources Act of 1982 was overtly full of holes. The act made owners on 186 specific strips of undeveloped land ineligible for federal subsidies because they were so vulnerable to storm damage or general erosion—but thousands of other disasters were still waiting to happen, with officials waiting to send checks.

After Hurricane Hugo devastated South Carolina in 1989, engineers criticized government officials for enabling low-quality construction in a high-hazard area. In 1992 the Congressional Research Service labeled federal disaster relief "an entitlement program" that creates "a potentially expensive arrangement"—quite a remarkable understatement by the author. Words like that were heard again thirteen years later in the aftermath of Hurricane Katrina, but none of that debate was truly new, not even for the Bush family. When Hurricane Andrew caused huge damage in Florida in 1992, Dade County officials on television screamed that President George H. W. Bush didn't care. During a futile reelection attempt, Bush promised Floridians a multibillion-dollar moon over Miami, including the rebuilding of Homestead Air Force Base at a time when other, intact bases were being closed.

Not only the feds have faltered. After Hurricane Andrew struck with a record bill estimated at $35 billion, Florida officials, in 1993, formed the Florida Residential Property and Casualty Joint Underwriting Association (RPC-JUA), which deliberately underpriced insurance. Their goal was to keep insurance prices "affordable" in South Florida at a time when insurance companies reeling with heavy payouts wanted to dramatically raise rates or get out of the state entirely. Tallahassee politicians decreed that the insurance companies would be liable, in proportion to their market share, for any deficits the JUA ran.

Unsurprisingly, the JUA rapidly became the second largest underwriter of homeowner policies in the state, and more private insurers tried to hustle out of Florida before they would be stuck with the bill. The Musulin study in 1997 showed that primary beneficiaries of the subsidized premiums, designed to promote affordable housing, were wealthy individuals. That's not surprising, because property owners close to the coast are at greater risk, and household income is related to proximity to the coast.

Federal disaster declarations marched to a faster beat during the Clinton administration, even as the number of warnings also grew. In 1993 the National Academy of Public Administration questioned the proliferation of disaster declarations, arguing that "state and local governments must be able to successfully manage small- and medium-sized disasters on their own." In 1994 the Northridge, California, earthquake broke Hurricane Andrew's two-year-old national record, with losses estimated at $44 billion.

FEMA's reaction to that earthquake helped it to cement its Lady Bountiful reputation of flinging coins from the carriage. Reporter James Bovard found that FEMA began mailing checks out to homeowners even before they had claimed a dime's worth of damage. All it took to get an average grant of $3,450 was an address in the proper ZIP code. Officials granted $142 million in "fast-track assistance" to people who collected without having their homes undergo any type of inspection.

The staggering costs made even some in Washington blink. In 1994 the House Bipartisan Natural Disasters Task Force observed: "If state and local governments believe that the federal government will meet their needs in every disaster, they have less incentive to spend scarce state and local resources on disaster preparedness, mitigation, response, and recovery. This not only raises the costs of disasters to federal taxpayers, but also to our society as a whole as people are encouraged to take risks they think they will not have to pay for."

In 1995 a Senate Bipartisan Task Force on Funding Disaster Relief stated that "FEMA has no method for evaluating the capabilities of the state and local governments" to respond to disasters. The task force forecasted that federal disaster costs would explode unless Congress established clearer and more stringent criteria for providing disaster assistance, along with incentives to reduce hazard and rely more on private insurance, and established a policy of offsetting expenses by cuts in other spending. That year also the Association of State Floodplain Managers stated that disaster relief "policies have enticed additional development increasing the damage potential for severe floods." The association went on to say, "With a benevolent federal government, there has been little incentive at the local and state levels of government to minimize the creation of new hazards."

The Clinton administration certainly heard this repetitive chorus. Vice President Al Gore, as part of his Reinventing Government program, chaired a National Performance Review on FEMA: the NPR report stated that criteria for presidential disaster declarations were unclear and noted that "the ready availability of federal funds may actually contribute to disaster losses by reducing incentives for hazard mitigation and preparedness." The result was that FEMA underwent another reorganization and announced in 1995 that one of its main goals was to "reduce the loss of life, property, and the environment [*sic*] by 50 percent over the next twenty-five years."

RECENT INNOVATIONS

During the decade after that goal setting, U.S. policy headed in the opposite direction, with politics a major culprit: President Clinton was spectacular at public emoting, to the extent that "I feel your pain" became one of his signature lines. In 1992 President Bush had reacted politically to Hurricane Andrew, yet his successor went much further during the election year of 1996 and declared disaster not the standard two-thirds of the time that requests came in but 85 percent of the time. That percentage yielded seventy-five disasters, about one for every five days in 1996—at that time, a record.

The Clinton administration also became the first to call snowstorms national disasters. After the first year of such practice, even the Gore-originated National Performance Review was indignant: "The system as a whole encourages state and local elected officials to ask for maximum federal disaster assistance . . . minor emergencies have been awarded full compensation. The federal government expects to pay seventeen states and the District of Columbia a total of $126 million for the costs of snow removal . . . after the March 1993 storms, even though snow is a regular, recurring event in many of the affected states."

Despite such scorn, President Clinton turned snowstorms into federal disasters ten times a year during his first term. The Clinton administration used not only a shotgun approach of disaster aid for virtually anyone who asked but a politically lasered approach as well. When California, with its prime collection of electoral votes, suffered from floods in 1995, President Clinton included each of the state's counties (with one exception) in his disaster declaration and waived the general requirement to conduct preliminary damage assessments in each county before passing out checks.

Occasionally the Clinton administration tried to rein in runaway programs. In 1998 FEMA urged Congress to stop funding the Corps of Engineers' program to replace beaches eroded by storms, arguing that the program encouraged people to live too close to the shore. Congress rejected the request, and one speaker at the National Hurricane Conference that year, Raymond Burby, said with exasperation, "The federal government has made it foolish (in fact, to seem like a sucker) for local government and individuals to take steps to avoid catastrophic losses in hurricanes." What insurance companies term "moral hazard"—policies that lead property owners into the temptation to be negligent—had become systematic.

What welfare produced in the inner city, the federal disaster program created for those living in risky areas. Fifty years of increasing payouts suggested that anyone who did not take what Uncle Sam offered was a chump. In 2001 the Bush administration ambitiously started off trying to force state and local officials to think twice before opening the spigot, by cutting the federal share from 75 percent (and higher when politics dictated) to 50 percent. But Senator John Edwards (D-NC) was one of many from southeastern coastal states and California to protest: "The disaster-response program is critically important. . . . You can't just put this burden on the state government. They just can't carry the burden by themselves."

Given how badly local and state muscles had deteriorated from years of respite from heavy lifting, he may have had a point. FEMA director Joe Allbaugh, a capable administrator, started off aggressively. When Davenport, Iowa, flooded and requests for federal aid poured in, Allbaugh said that the city fathers had been irresponsible: "How many times will the American taxpayer have to step in and take care of this flooding, which could easily have been prevented by building levees and dikes?" In congressional testimony he equated federal disaster assistance with "an oversized entitlement program and a disincentive to effective state and local risk management."

For that truth telling he received castigation and eventually left FEMA. His successor was Michael Brown, and the rest was hysteria.

Part Two

WHAT WENT RIGHT

Those facing disaster need four kinds of help. First, to become survivors, they sometimes need *rescue* from rising water, surging fire, or collapsed buildings. Second, they often need immediate *relief*, since they are often separated from their regular ways of accessing food, water, shelter, clothing, and power. Third, once the days of emergency are over, they need *recovery* over the subsequent weeks and months. They need their usual income plus perhaps more to do repairs, but their regular means of receiving income may have vanished. Fourth, as material needs are met, they also need psychological and spiritual *restoration*, because their previous bedrock may have been sundered by physical and emotional earthquakes.

Back-to-back Associated Press stories on September 6 cited two different ways of offering Katrina relief. One story from Lancaster, Pennsylvania, that moved on the wire at 7:00 p.m. reported: "Twenty adults and nineteen children showed up at Patricia and Timothy Edwards' house a few hours before dawn Sunday, and now it's their home, even if some have to sleep four to a bed. . . . Patricia Edwards, a New Orleans native who works as a machinist in a Lancaster candy factory, opened her home to all her extended family after her seventy-two-year-old mother Beatrice Duplessis told her they had nowhere to turn. 'I said, "Wait a minute, stop right now." I didn't think twice: "Bring them all, I don't care,"' she said.'

The next story came at 7:02 p.m.: "Hundreds of firefighters have been sitting in Atlanta, playing cards and taking FEMA history classes, instead of doing what they came to do: help hurricane victims. The volunteers traveled south and west from around the country. . . . They came after FEMA put out a call for two thousand firefighters to help with community service. Firefighters arrived, as told, with lifesaving equipment and sleeping bags." They then spent two days doing paperwork and sitting through FEMA courses on diversity and sexual harassment: "The FEMA director in charge of fire fighters says he's trying to get the volunteers deployed ASAP, but wants to make sure they go to the right place. One firefighter points to nightly reports of hurricane victims asking how they were forgotten. He says, 'we didn't forget, we're stuck in Atlanta drinking beer.'"

Chapter 4

RESCUE AND RELIEF

While many politicians and reporters fiddled and diddled during the Katrina disaster, four groups responded well: individual volunteers, military personnel, business employees, and volunteers with religious organizations. The volunteer and military first responders helped the Katrina death total end up a little over one thousand in Louisiana, as compared to the ten thousand Mayor Nagin predicted or the sixty thousand forecasted by a computer model. The number of those helped was huge: based on one *Washington Post* survey of survivors, the rescuers brought to safety forty to fifty thousand people, including some who had been caught in attics with the water almost over their heads.

The volunteer heroes included hundreds of people who set out on their boats from regular docking places or from spots on the new rivers that ran through the streets of New Orleans. Some used their trucks or SUVs to haul boats to interstate off-ramps, then launched from there. These rescuers weren't ordered to their posts by FEMA, the governor, or the mayor. They often acted on their own, as did other civilian rescue teams, and as did some police and over a hundred firefighters when ruptured communications left them with no commands but those of their own conscience.

Few journalists knew or reported this story: the Louisiana Department of Wildlife and Fisheries—which sent out agents on boats, loosely coordinated volunteer rescue efforts, and claimed twenty thousand rescues—wasn't on press call lists. Former reporter and firefighter Lou Dolinar later wrote that this volunteer response "was immediate and massive—it just wasn't the response the media wanted, expected, or was spoon-fed at a press conference." He went on to say, "[Since] there was no central clearinghouse for information on rescue efforts, what looked like a hurricane relief breakdown was in fact a press release breakdown."

Volunteers also were important in the relief efforts that followed rescues. During the week after Katrina hit, thousands of people filled online listings offering help: "I am a licensed bus driver willing to go south to haul those folks out." "I am a house painter." "I am fully licensed, have a truck with all equipment and chemicals, and am willing to go down and help out with any pest control problems." "I'm a building and roofing contractor from upstate New York who will donate my expertise and labor." "I am background-screened and fingerprinted for childcare, willing to take in a few kids or a small family." "I speak fluent Spanish and will contact anyone for anybody."

Some of those people never carried through on their initial impulse, but many did, including some from among the medical personnel who wrote of their willingness to serve: "I'm a board certified orthopedic surgeon who is willing to help in a medical capacity." "I am a nurse from Cleveland." "I am a fully licensed general surgery chief resident willing to help immediately." "I am a CPR-certified health-care provider." Some specialists were willing to be generalists: "Hi—I'm a registered nurse, my boyfriend is a union electrician. Even if you couldn't use us in our professions, we would be willing to provide any assistance necessary."

Many people offered housing, and some had their offers accepted: "Can't get out there myself, but we have a dry, clean living room with space for a small family and their pets." "We only have our hearts and our home to offer, but our home is comfortable and dry!" "I am a single mother with a small baby at home. I have an extra room and can house a single parent and/or children. It's not a lot of space, but I can help with meals, clothing, employment, and schooling." "We are licensed, loving foster parents who would be honored to take in a baby/toddler/young child—short or long term."

Many people without special training or available space just offered themselves: "I was down at Ground Zero after 9/11 and can help with any manual labor, rebuilding, medical help, search and rescue, and anything else under the sun." "I cannot offer my apartment for shelter at this time because I have no power/water, and I cannot offer money because I have very little, but I am very able to help out physically." "I have two Husky chain saws, transportation, and complete camping and cooking gear. No pay required, just a destination and a person who truly needs help."

Hundreds of stories emerged like this one from *Beliefnet* about a person who was feeling helpless watching Hurricane Katrina coverage on television: "I said a prayer, 'Lord, I am giving money, but I want to do something personally. Send me someone to help.' About fifteen minutes later my phone rang. My neighbor said, 'We are helping seventy-five evacuees who are moving into a camp near Pell City, Alabama. Do you want to help?' 'YES,' I said. My husband and I moved into high gear. We gathered up linens, pillows, blankets, comforters, hair dryers, hot rollers, toiletries, makeup, soap, tools, clothing, fifteen pairs of shoes, etc. I am giving Wal-Mart gift certificates to hand out as well. It was such a joy for us to be able to share what God had blessed us with to help someone who had nothing."

Some volunteer actions even turned fear into hope, at least momentarily. The *New Orleans Times-Picayune* reported that as evacuation buses finally arrived at the Convention Center on Saturday, September 3, one woman, Anita Roach, "raised her voice to the heavens, belting out the gospel standards that had comforted her since childhood. . . .'When the storm of life is raging, Stand by me, stand by me. . . . ' Roach never stopped singing, never stopped smiling, never stopped comforting a crowd of some of the last of Hurricane Katrina's victims to receive even a shred of assistance. She sang from her belly with a voice that could be heard down the block. . . . One by one, family, friends, and complete strangers joined her, clapping and singing: 'When this world is tossing me like a ship on the raging sea, Thou who rulest the winds and water stand by me, stand by me.'"

Television viewers abroad may have seen images of helplessness, but many would-be volunteers showed a can-do spirit: "I can run heavy equipment or operate off-road vehicles and a variety of boats in highly variable and adverse conditions. I have extensive experience in the coastal marshes and swamps of south Louisiana and Mississippi and have construction, oil-field, and welding experience. I can also cook. I'll do anything to help, and I can bring some supplies."

MILITARY HEROES

Some of those volunteers had anarchic tendencies, but they ended up cooperating with highly disciplined professionals from the second group that made a difference—the military. Think of a team like the characters played by Mel Gibson and Danny Glover in *Lethal Weapon*, a madman and an honest cop: those were the heroes of this battle of New Orleans. Some of the professionals were a bit of both: Coast Guard and Louisiana National Guard helicopter flyers swooped in even before the hurricane winds had subsided, coming in low past twisted power lines.

Mayor Nagin had visited the Convention Center and then escaped from what he thought was danger, but the Coast Guard's top official on the scene, Rear Adm. Bob Duncan, flew in with the first crews. The Coast Guard used fifty helicopters and hundreds of boats to rescue twenty-four thousand people by its count, including perhaps four thousand from rooftops, and to move nine thousand of the most vulnerable from hospitals and nursing homes. Barges rescued hundreds of people stranded on broken levees.

Sometimes heroes encountered heroes, men in danger who stayed on a roof so a helicopter would have room for women and children. When there was no room for all, the stranded made sure that those in the worst shape were evacuated. Lou Dolinar described the flexibility displayed by crews of the Black Hawk helicopters: "Lacking rescue hoists, crews adopted the nervy tactic of landing directly on rooftops to take on passengers, while applying power to keep the helicopters light so they wouldn't collapse the storm-weakened buildings."

Other helicopters flew from the navy vessel *Bataan* and from National Guard units. Civilian search-and-rescue teams from out of state soon showed up, as did a volunteer squad from ExxonMobil. Choppers based at Naval Air Station Pensacola and elsewhere searched for survivors. When evening came crews used night-vision goggles to look for the flickering candles, flashlights, or lanterns of survivors. They rescued hundreds, including an elderly man with emphysema who had been trapped in his home for six days.

Most journalists paid little attention to these efforts, but *Connecticut Post* columnist Peter Urban reported that a single thirty-passenger Black Hawk of the Louisiana National Guard, on that first Monday, brought about two hundred fifty people to safety; the unit included sixteen other thirty-passenger Black Hawks, all stripped of seating to fly similar rescue missions. *World* reported that soon after the hurricane, Lt. Sean Maloney's helicopter was "plucking people off rooftops," and one-hundred-foot-long Marine Corps helicopters from North Carolina carried out up to fifty evacuees at a time. Paratroopers from the Army's 82nd Airborne Division hunted for survivors using inflatable Zodiac craft.

Many notable stories of military dedication also emerged. Nearly one hundred of the six hundred fifty people in one Seabee unit, Naval Mobile Construction Battalion 7, lost everything they owned. Still, day after day Seabees with heavy equipment, power tools, and the know-how to move or build almost anything headed out to other people's homes to yank trees off roofs, build tent cities, or rig up water pumps to get the dialysis machines running again.

Some politicians complained that boots on the ground could have come sooner, but Lt. Gen. H. Steven Blum explained to reporters why National Guard troops did not sweep into the city before Friday of hurricane week: "We waited until we had enough force in place to do an overwhelming force.... Had we gone in with less force, it may have been challenged, innocents may have been caught in a fight between the Guard military police and those who did not want to be processed or apprehended, and we would put innocents' lives at risk." Those (imaginary) massive bands of murderers and rapists slowed down relief.

Nevertheless, the overall Katrina effort was the fastest massive military response to any hurricane ever. The Pentagon committed to hurricane help about forty thousand troops, one hundred fifty aircraft, and a dozen ships, including the carrier *Truman*, the amphibious ships *Iwo Jima*, *Tortuga*, *Shreveport*, and *Whidbey Island*, and the high-speed catamaran *Swift*. The one part of the federal government that did function well amid the Katrina crisis was the military.

COMPANIES COMING THROUGH

Many large corporations also came through, with Wal-Mart making the biggest impact. While Katrina was still classified as a tropical storm on August 23, six days before it hit New Orleans, Wal-Mart's emergency operations center in Bentonville, Arkansas, was tracking it. Soon workers were shipping bottled water, flashlights, batteries, tarps, canned tuna, Strawberry Pop-Tarts (ready to eat, taste good), and other items to stores likely to be affected. Once Katrina hit, Wal-Mart's prepositioning of satellite phones and truckloads of water allowed it to deliver supplies faster than any governmental organization. It quickly sent nineteen hundred trailer loads of emergency supplies to afflicted areas, using its network of 126 facilities in the Gulf region.

Wal-Mart also allowed its managers to make decisions without requiring abundant paperwork. The comanager of Wal-Mart in Waveland, Mississippi, where floodwaters within the store were two feet deep and refrigerators and shelves were knocked over, had her stepbrother use a bulldozer to clear a path through the debris. She passed around socks, shoes, and dry underwear to barefoot neighbors and wet police officers. She handed out bottled water and sausages that had been stored high and gave insulin and drugs to AIDS patients.

Other stories also displayed initiative rather than rule by paperocracy. In one Jefferson Parish store just outside New Orleans, an employee used a forklift to open the warehouse door to deliver water to stranded elderly residents. Wal-Mart's Bentonville headquarters phone bank, first set up to help displaced employees, soon became the go-to operation for others who had no success with government bureaucracy. For example, Wal-Mart helped a New Orleans couple find their newborn child, who had been moved to a Houston neonatal center.

The result was a wave of rave reviews by local officials. Sheriff Harry Lee spoke about conditions in his Jefferson Parish, just outside of New Orleans: "FEMA executives were there, but they didn't do anything. They weren't up and running for four or five days. . . . If the federal government would have responded as quickly as Wal-Mart, we could have saved more lives." Lee said FEMA made things worse rather than better: When Wal-Mart sent three trailer trucks with water to a FEMA compound, "much to my dismay, FEMA turned them away. . . . They said they didn't need it." FEMA officials said they needed written authorization—paperocracy!—to accept such supplies and didn't have any. Wal-Mart distributed the water directly.

Philip Capitano, the mayor of one Jefferson Parish city, Kenner, said Wal-Mart arrived days before FEMA: "The only lifeline in Kenner was the Wal-Mart stores. We didn't have looting on a mass scale because Wal-Mart showed up with food and water." He added, "FEMA needs to take a master class in logistics and mobilization from Wal-Mart." A resident of Jefferson Parish said on the September 4 *Meet the Press*, "If the American government would have responded like Wal-Mart . . . we wouldn't be in this crisis."

Some local broadcast stories starred "Wal-Mart angels," and a few journalists drew logical lessons from business success. *Denver Post* columnist David Harsanyi noted that since government failed: "Why is the near-universal solution from pundits and officials to propose more government? Will we ever learn? . . . Judging by the results of Hurricane Katrina, we'd do ourselves a favor by hiring nongovernmental entities such as Wal-Mart," which had trucks getting into disaster areas before official relief workers did. *Fortune* flared a headline "The Only Lifeline Was the Wal-Mart," and dubbed Wal-Mart "an operation that could teach FEMA a thing or two."

The home-improvement chain Home Depot also reacted like Wal-Mart, although on a smaller scale. It tracked buying patterns after past storms and stocked supplies customers would want. It dispatched generators, flashlights, batteries, and lumber to distribution areas just outside where Katrina was expected to hit. Home Depot loaded fifty trucks with supplies in Houston and Tallahassee so employees could head to stricken areas as soon as the hurricane passed. The company was flexible enough to go beyond the usual inventories and have food and diapers available. It also had five hundred employees from neighboring states waiting in hotels ready to staff Home Depot stores in case regular workers couldn't make it or extra hands were needed.

Home Depot, like Wal-Mart, emphasized performance, not paperocracy —but sometimes it had to do social work. Paul Raines, president of Home Depot's Southern division, said shortly after the hurricane hit: "At this point, customers are in shock. They don't know what to do after a storm, so we have to help them. In the early stages, they're looking to put a tarp up, get a cover over a window, drain some water, just basically get some shelter. Right now, it's very immediate—chain saws, generators, water. Roofing shingles and major construction come a lot later."

FedEx also responded well, which FedEx division head Dave Bronczek said was not surprising: "That's the nature of our business. We're used to dealing with crisis." *Fortune* described the company's style: "At any given moment, somewhere in the world there is a social upheaval, a dangerous storm, a wildcat strike. . . . FedEx, which earns its money by being dependable, can't afford a wait-and-see attitude; it moves in advance."

To be prepared, FedEx does more disaster drills than FEMA, anticipating earthquakes, bioterrorism, or "a monster typhoon hitting the company's hub in the Philippines." Before Katrina hit, FedEx positioned thirty thousand bags of ice, thirty thousand gallons of water, and eighty-five home generators outside Baton Rouge and Tallahassee so that it could move in quickly after the storm to help employees. The company also worked with the Red Cross, delivering five hundred tons of relief supplies, mostly at no charge. FedEx also keeps at its hubs shipping containers filled with bandages, blankets, and batteries, so that material can be sent quickly to any disaster site.

If we compare *F* to *F*, FedEx to FEMA, it's clear that one was galloping and one was limping. William Carwile, then FEMA's top responder in

Mississippi, complained in a September 2 e-mail message to Washington officials that substandard levels of food, water, and ice were being distributed in Mississippi: "System appears broken. . . . There seems to be no way we will get commodities in amounts beyond those indicated below. And it turns out these shortfalls were known much earlier in the day and we were not informed." FedEx's execs knew what was going on from hour to hour.

Wal-Mart, Home Depot, and FedEx were the big three among companies reacting to Katrina, but many others helped in their own ways. General Electric put together a team of fifty project engineers with expertise in portable water purification, medical equipment, and energy. UPS helped FEMA to direct people and supplies. Pfizer sent drugs into devastated areas and helped government agencies, hospitals, and retailers to establish systems for storing and distributing drugs to evacuees. Georgia Pacific sent paper plates, napkins, and toilet paper.

Cingular was ready with hundreds of emergency generators to power cell towers shut down when electricity failed. Insurers flew in extra personnel and set up hotlines to process claims. Other companies suspended monthly mortgage or car payments. Small businesses also pitched in, with the U.S. Chamber of Commerce's nonprofit Center for Corporate Citizenship becoming a clearinghouse that took calls and compiled lists of needed supplies. Donor companies avoided tie-ups or duplication by agreeing to fill specific requests.

Rather than citing more individual companies, let's now turn to the fourth group that received praise after Katrina hit: faith-based organizations. Ronnie Harris, mayor of the New Orleans suburb of Gretna, flat-out said, "Church workers were the first volunteers on the ground." Others during the Katrina relief effort concurred, as volunteers from the Salvation Army, Operation Blessing, the Southern Baptist Convention, and many other groups helped by providing thousands of beds, serving millions of meals, and dishing up spiritual perspective and comfort as well, as the next chapter will show.

Chapter 5

RELIEF AND RECOVERY

Some say the government's job is so big and its funds so vast that any comparison of religious and governmental aid programs is comparing grapes to watermelons. And yet the big numbers compiled during the two months after Katrina suggest otherwise. Nine thousand Southern Baptists from forty-one states volunteered 120,000 days during which they served 10 million meals and pushed forward cleanup and recovery efforts. During those same two months the Salvation Army served nearly 5 million hot meals and more than 6.5 million sandwiches, snacks, and drinks from 178 mobile feeding units and eleven field kitchens, with each kitchen able to produce twenty thousand hot meals per day.

The Salvation Army rotated into the disaster area twelve thousand employees and twenty-eight thousand volunteers on two-week shifts, and also distributed one hundred fifty-eight thousand cleaning kits (broom, bucket, mop, detergent) and one hundred thirty thousand boxes of groceries, assisting in this process about one million individuals. As the *Wall Street Journal* reported, "The Salvation Army's daily work in permanent shelters with the homeless and poor and with people trying to put their lives back together after an apartment fire or years of alcohol and drug abuse helps." The *Journal* quoted the Salvation Army's Maj. George Hood: "We do this extremely well because we are already there 365 days a year serving the poorest of the poor in these communities. We are serving many of the same clients, but now they don't have homes."

Other groups, such as Operation Blessing, delivered food, blankets, and generators to evacuee-sheltering churches. These organizations showed greater flexibility than did government organizations ruled by paperocracy. For example, Houston pastor David Pittman observed, "Many of the evacuees had moved into apartments with little or no furniture. I thought that maybe one of the greatest needs would probably be a 'good night's rest' in order to function as best as possible when facing trials and tough decisions in their daily rigorous routine." Pittman's group, The Rock Ministries, provided mattresses to numerous families.

Many who were helped also rated the dedication of church volunteers as higher than that of the government workers. Southern Baptist volunteer coordinator Bob Reccord explained, "For people who are employed with disaster relief, it is to some degree a job. For volunteer faith-based people, it is a passion and a sense of calling." Reccord also spoke of the flexibility of groups outside the paperocracy, saying that his operation's response time made it a "speedboat" in comparison to the government's "battleship."

Hundreds of churches had stories like this one from Gautier Presbyterian Church in Gautier, Mississippi, which helped a disabled veteran who learned that Veterans Administration protocols did not allow it to replace the dentures, eyeglasses, and hearing aids swept away by Katrina. Church volunteers raised money to cover the dentures, prepaid a Wal-Mart optician's bill, and took him to the VA to meet with a patient's advocate to push harder on getting the hearing aid. When church volunteers spotted an elderly lady living in a tent beside her ruined home, they immediately obtained for her food, blankets, a generator, a lamp, and an electric heater, and then pressed for a long-term solution.

Groups often worked together. At Long Beach, Mississippi, Southern Baptist Disaster Relief volunteers from Ohio, Iowa, Tennessee, and Kentucky joined the Salvation Army for a mass feeding operation in the parking lot of a tattered Piggly Wiggly. The volunteers in yellow hats worked in mid-nineties heat distributing meals in the parking lot or loading Salvation Army canteen trucks. The trucks carried meals to Gulfport and other decimated towns, often sharing gas with the local sheriff's department.

Nor did Katrina exhaust many of the apparently indefatigable volunteers. When Wilma, late in the hurricane season, left 3.2 million residents in southern Florida not only waterlogged but powerless, Christian groups were once again handing out water, ice, food, roof tarps, and generators. At one site, when Operation Blessing needed more volunteer help, its team called Mennonites in Alabama: fifteen immediately set out, driving all night to set up a mobile kitchen and serve hot meals with food delivered by Operation Blessing trucks.

When electricity did not come back on in many retirement communities with large Jewish populations, synagogues also became active. Temple Emeth, a two-thousand-member synagogue located within a mile of the twelve-thousand-resident Kings Point complex in Delray Beach, organized relief efforts. Jeffrey Willens, administrator of Temple Sinai a half mile down the road, called the elderly members of his temple to see what they required: "In some cases they just needed some human contact, so we provided that too." Other Jewish groups participated in Katrina relief.

Some Islamic groups also became involved. The Muslim American Society sent to New Orleans medical teams made up of Muslims from Houston, Baton Rouge, Boston, and Tampa. In Houston so many religious groups volunteered to help New Orleans evacuees at the Astrodome and other sites that officials used a random drawing to assign dates, and the Houston Muslim community ended up with . . . September 11. Parvez Ahmed, chairman of the board of the Council on American-Islamic Relations, said he welcomed the "opportunity to dispel myths about Islam and terrorism."

REFUSALS TO GIVE UP

Numerous individual stories in *World* gave a glimpse of the whole:

- One sixty-six-year-old leader in the Southern Baptist Disaster Relief network, Travis Maynard, was on the move week after week during September in a way that did not make his cardiologist happy. Three years before, while Maynard was undergoing chemotherapy and radiation to treat cancer, he had a massive heart attack. But as he headed up a twenty-four-person crew capable of serving ten thousand to sixteen thousand meals a day, he refused to stop, saying, "I'm here to serve. This is my calling."

- Nearly 10 percent of the congregation of Pass Road Baptist Church in Gulfport lost everything, but the church staged a relief effort that included volunteers from North Carolina preparing and serving meals, and those from Pensacola, Florida, setting up a mobile medical clinic they had brought.

- Darrin Curtis, with his wife and two children, left his home in Chalmette, Lousiana, and ended up with two hundred fifty other evacuees in the gym of Faith Presbyterian Church in Brookhaven, Mississippi. He reported that his house was under fifteen feet of water, and everything material he had was gone. The church helped him find a job as a carpenter, and he planned to stay. "Why would I want to go anywhere else?"

- Thousands of evacuees ended up in Jackson, Mississippi, where First Baptist Church became a shelter for people with special medical needs. Dozens of cots and a handful of hospital beds soon lined the church's gym, with some taken by the elderly, creating a makeshift clinic run by volunteer nurses and doctors. One eighty-three-year-old, Thomas Smith, had missed two critical dialysis treatments in New Orleans before he was airlifted to Jackson and to First Baptist, where he said volunteers treated him better than doctors back home.

- In Biloxi, Samaritan's Purse set up camp at a United Methodist conference center that escaped destruction. One of the volunteers there, San Diego firefighter Rusty Thill, had sold everything in his apartment when he heard the Katrina news; he then drove his Chevy truck to the Gulf Coast. From there he went every day on missions, such as one that took him to the home of Linda Ogden and her elderly mother. He and other volunteers lay sturdy tarps on Ms. Ogden's leaking roof, an effort that left her in wonder: "I can't believe they would help people for free like this. I'm so thankful."

- In Central Texas, Great Hills Baptist Church of Austin and the Southern Baptist Convention coordinated mercy flights by pilots who donated their time and planes to ship provisions to flooded areas. "Load it up, fly it over, and stay long enough to pick up some fuel," said pilot Derrich Pollock of Austin.

Cable news channels focused on complainers rather than on Lee and Sharon Sandifer, members of Slidell Bible Chapel in Louisiana, who lost everything material after Katrina's fifteen-foot storm surge washed through their residence. They hauled the waterlogged contents to the street and posted a sign: "This pile of stuff was not our life, our life is hid in Christ."

Also receiving little play were testimonies like Joan Hampton's at the Austin Convention Center. There she told a reporter that although she arrived with only her "work uniform and four Bibles in a plastic bag," she was thankful. Hampton sat on her new bed surrounded by chairs, which she had arranged into a cubby of personal space, and said: "I am home. I am surrounded by love." Although Katrina destroyed her New Orleans house, she was grateful for what she still had: "I didn't lose anything. The Lord has blessed me." She planned to spend the day writing down in a notebook all she had seen.

The experiences of evacuees varied enormously, and not only by their physical surroundings; their interior dispositions were crucial. For example, the *Washington Times* reported the story of Joseph Brant, a black hitchhiker out of New Orleans who rode with a van of white folks to Houston.

The long trip took a big bite out of his lifelong distrust of whites, and the following Sunday he was praising God and exulting that the experience "changed me forever." Others came to smaller but still useful revelations. One thirty-six-year-old, Traci Saucier, said that the experience "makes you realize how much you take for granted, like air conditioning, being able to eat what you want." She said, "Stuff you think is an everyday thing is really a luxury, like having cable and Internet and being able to wash your hair every day."

Again and again in Florida and in the area surrounding New Orleans, the absence of paperocracy made a crucial difference in the speed of delivering assistance. At Shiloh Baptist Church in Baton Rouge, pastor's wife and relief coordinator Eula Smith said, "We have not had to worry about any red tape, so we have been able to be quick." Senator Rick Santorum (R-PA) reported, "You don't hear the complaints about . . . the red tape, the bureaucracy, and the inefficiency in the nonprofit sector, particularly the faith-based sector, the churches, who were out there on the front line meeting needs."

COMPARISONS WITH GOVERNMENT

Government aid, meanwhile, almost always seemed to come too little and too late, or (when unfavorable publicity arose) flung to some in need but to many in greed. Even the *New York Times* reported that in November 2005, when FEMA with the Red Cross decided to give out $62 million in aid in Jackson, Mississippi, to people who said their homes were uninhabitable, FEMA overlooked a critical fact: "The storm was hardly catastrophic here, one hundred sixty miles from the coast. The only damage sustained by most of the nearly thirty thousand households receiving aid was spoiled food in the freezer." With FEMA not conducting any home inspections, the *Times* reported, "payments of up to $2,358 set off spending sprees on jewelry, guns and electronics."

After the folly came the cover-up. FEMA had sent checks to 7,622 Jackson-area residents who said their homes were ruined, but county emergency director Larry J. Fisher counted only about fifty uninhabitable homes. FEMA told Fisher to resolve the discrepancy by increasing his number to four thousand, but the sixty-seven-year-old Baptist deacon and former city police detective refused to revise his reports. Meanwhile, one thousand reports of fraud emerged, including accusations that people lied about damage claims and falsified their addresses.

The Jackson area was not the only place where fraud seemed evident. In Iberia Parish, west of New Orleans, perhaps three mobile homes were damaged, but FEMA sent 404 families $2,000 checks as emergency aid.

Senator Susan M. Collins (R-ME), whose committee oversees FEMA, expressed her frustration: "FEMA seems incapable of paying legitimate claims quickly and effectively and yet reimburses fraudulent claims without asking any questions. It is the worst of all worlds."

This worst of worlds was nothing new for FEMA, which gave $29 million in flood relief to Mobile, Alabama, after Hurricane Andrew in 1992, even though local officials said there was no damage. A federal audit revealed officials after other disasters using funds for European vacationing. In 2004 after Hurricane Frances, FEMA distributed $31 million to Miami area residents, even though Frances skirted the city and caused damage consisting largely of some downed telephone poles.

That last dispersal drew the ire of the *Fort Lauderdale Sun-Sentinel*, which found that FEMA paid Miamians for 5,000 televisions, 1,440 air conditioners, 1,360 twin beds, 1,311 washers and dryers, and 831 dining sets—all purported to be damaged by Frances. The *Sun-Sentinel* also found that thirty of one hundred thirty inspectors hired by FEMA to assess hurricane damage had criminal backgrounds, and one trainer of inspectors had served six years in prison in three different states for criminal sexual conduct, attempted embezzlement of public money, conspiracy to commit wire fraud, and cocaine possession.

So post-Katrina embarrassments came as no surprise, and stories began to emerge quickly: the *New York Daily News* reported that debit cards distributed by FEMA were being used in "luxury goods stores as far away as Atlanta." The *New Orleans Times-Picayune* reported federally contracted truck drivers looting items including toys and lingerie. The criticism of big governmental relief efforts came with unusual praise for churches in headlines like this one from the *New York Times*: "A New Meaning for 'Organized Religion': It Helps the Needy Quickly." The story described how "from sprawling megachurches to tiny congregations, churches across the country have mobilized in response to Hurricane Katrina, offering shelter, conducting clothing drives and serving hot meals to evacuees, many of whom have had difficulty getting help from inundated government agencies."

The details got to *Times* reporters Michael Luo and Campbell Robertson: "The main hallway of the Florida Boulevard Baptist Church is lined with garbage bags full of clothing. The gymnasium has become a soup kitchen. And a kitchen set up outside churns out several thousand hot meals a day. At River of Praise Church in Tomball, Texas, one hundred fifty evacuees from the New Orleans area are camped out on cots in the family activity room, two youth rooms and a conference room." The *Times* contrasted help to those in need with paperocracy, quoting one evacuee from the Ninth Ward, fifty-seven-year-old Ethel Wicker: "You just walk in. They have clothing. . . . And they treat you very well." In contrast, she spoke of waiting for hours to get food stamps and receiving nothing from FEMA.

The federal government, it seemed, was the bad kind of father, alternately a bully and a pantywaist, with little in between. Sometimes, as in Jackson, FEMA merely passed out the money to people without demanding any evidence. But those who had truly suffered learned—as the *Times* summarized the message from FEMA spokesman David G. Passey—that they needed to "register for assistance, and that checks or funds transfers would usually take between ten days and two weeks to reach them." The *Times* continued, "Many people said they could not wait that long, or did not have the patience to deal with all the bureaucratic mix-ups."

THE FALL OF THE RED CROSS

One major nonprofit that began with a Christian sensibility but lost it while becoming intertwined with the federal government, the American Red Cross, garnered disdain similar to that aimed at Washington. The *New York Times*, in December 2005, summarized the criticism of the one relief organization that is federally chartered and included in the National Response Plan as the prime responder to catastrophes: "Victims and volunteers complained that the organization's response to the disaster was slow and tangled in red tape. Aid seekers described interminable busy signals on hotline numbers. Concerns about mismanagement heightened in October when the organization admitted it had wildly miscalculated the number of evacuees staying in hotels and motels around the country."

The gross overestimation stung. The Red Cross initially reported for purposes of government reimbursement that six hundred thousand evacuees were staying in hotels at a cost of about $11 million per night. When that figure received challenge, the Red Cross acknowledged that the real number was two hundred thousand at a cost of $4 million per night, and officials admitted that they had made several incorrect assumptions. One was that evacuees leaving shelters would head to government-paid hotel rooms at an average cost of $61 per night. However, many evacuees moved back to their homes, used funds to move into apartments, or found lodging with friends, relatives, or compassionate strangers.

The hotel gaffe was not the organization's only exaggeration. The Red Cross Web site late in October claimed that the organization had served twenty-five million meals at an average cost of five dollars per meal, but many of those were served by Southern Baptist Relief and other organizations. Red Cross spokeswoman Sarah Marchetti told the *New York Sun* that her organization had helped four million Katrina victims, but that number equals the entire population of greater New Orleans and all of Mississippi. Richard Walden, director of Operation USA, a smaller charity, estimated that the Red Cross had helped around three hundred thousand people.

Other criticisms of the Red Cross grew throughout the fall of 2005:

- The *Washington Post* reported: "Evacuees in rural communities waited days for the Red Cross to show up. Those who could find phones dialed for hours to reach a toll-free number set up to link them with Red Cross financial help. In Shreveport, Lousiana, the shelter in the Hirsch Coliseum was so short of basic supplies that Red Cross staff went begging to a local church for diapers and underwear."

- Tim Kellar, administrator of Hancock County, Mississippi (adjacent to Louisiana), said, "The Red Cross has been my biggest disappointment. I held it in such high esteem until we were in the time of need. It was nonexistent." County resident Betty Brunner, a Red Cross volunteer since 1969, said, "I will never, ever wear the Red Cross vest again."

- The *Wall Street Journal* reported that in East Biloxi, thirty miles eastward, the Salvation Army received massive applause at a community meeting and that the Red Cross received heckling, with one resident, Eula Crowell, asking a Red Cross official where the money is: "All these people across America are giving money over the TV. I would tell them to put it back in their pocket." Red Cross volunteer Susan Turner of East Biloxi said, "The Red Cross didn't do anything for us."

- Vernon Jones, chief executive of DeKalb County, Georgia, asked the Red Cross to leave a relief center for hurricane evacuees in suburban Atlanta. He said its paper application process was too tedious and that the group was falsely promising financial payments to shut up temporarily irate evacuees.

- George Penick, president of the Foundation for the Mid South, which helped coordinate relief efforts, said that the Red Cross was wasting money and at crucial times "was either absent or overwhelmed." He said, "You had churches and nonprofit groups taking care of the evacuees in any way they could with whatever money they could scrape together."

The criticism was bipartisan. Rep. Jim McCrery (R-LA) said that the Red Cross was not able to fulfill its mandated role as the lead provider of disaster aid. He offered this example: it took the Red Cross a week to supply $60,000 in new bedding donated by General Motors to a shelter in Natchitoches, where people displaced by the storm were sleeping on the floor. He said that the organization had suffered "an inexcusable breakdown": "After witnessing the American Red Cross's struggles during Katrina and Rita, I am not sure it is prudent for Congress to place such great responsibility in the hands of one organization."

Meanwhile, Rep. Bennie G. Thompson (D-MS) had his staffers produce a report raking the Red Cross and praising a religious group: "While the Red Cross waited to confirm the severity of the disaster, the Salvation Army was already on the ground working with local churches at the site." Thompson's crew went back fifteen years to assess how the Red Cross performed after floods in Alabama and Ohio and tornadoes in Indiana, and portrayed the organization as a haven for paper-pushing publicity seekers. The staffers charged that the Red Cross dispatched public relations personnel first to put up Red Cross banners and signs, then video crews, and only then aid workers, who required detailed reports before dispensing relief.

The Red Cross versus Salvation Army controversy received headline play in the *Wall Street Journal*: "Katrina Aid Stirs Unintended Rivalry?: Salvation Army Wins Hearts, Red Cross Faces Critics." The article noted, "The Salvation Army is drawing praise for its swift arrival in the most distressed areas and clearly winning the hearts of desperate residents. To some people here, the Red Cross, under growing criticism for letting bureaucratic hurdles slow down aid in the disaster area, suffers by comparison." Local residents traded stories about how the Red Cross would not set up a shelter in one school because it lacked a dehumidifier and would not bring food to some shelters because it was after dark. It seemed that Clara Barton's nineteenth-century fear concerning Red Cross's success was coming true: "If the Red Cross becomes too bureaucratic and businesslike, its compassion and effectiveness as a relief organization would diminish."

As criticism grew, other charities quietly complained that they did the work, Red Cross publicity teams took the credit, and the Red Cross got the donations. It gnaws at other relief leaders that for decades the federal government has played favorites, giving the Red Cross the paramount position in disaster relief and certifying it as the only nongovernmental organization mandated by Congress to provide aid. It has bothered them that the Red Cross received additional payments ($27 million in 2004) when, even with its favored fund-raising position, shortfalls have occurred. And it upset them that President Bush, in his major national address after Katrina, urged Americans to send cash to one organization: "The Red Cross needs our help. I urge our fellow citizens to contribute."

Such pleas, along with massive advertising by the Red Cross and its reputation as the paramount relief organization, were successful: of $2.7 billion donated for hurricane relief through November 21, 2005, the Red Cross received $1.52 billion, compared with $270 million for the distant second-place organization, the Salvation Army. But its established position is in jeopardy, with even the *New York Times* concluding, "The Red Cross is more interested in deflecting criticism than in improving its response to emergencies." The establishment clause of the First Amendment stopped any denomination from getting a favored federal position; it's time to do the same for charities by disestablishing the Red Cross.

PRESS REACTIONS

Praise from major newspapers for the Salvation Army and other evangelical efforts was unusual: Christians who aspire to a "Well done, good and faithful servant" headline in the *Times* rather than praise from God are both theologically confused and courting frustration. However, the contrast between charity and bureaucracy was too powerful to ignore. Astoundingly, even the ACLU and other groups that often shriek at religious activities in the public square offered only the sounds of silence when local and state officials asked church volunteers to take charge of post-Katrina feeding programs. Nor did they speak up when church members held worship services and passed out Bibles at government shelters like the George R. Brown Convention Center in Houston. Pastors prayed with evacuees, apparently thinking that they might need spiritual as well as material help.

The press largely ignored the lack of separation of church and state. One reporter who noted the religious involvement quoted New Orleans evacuees such as Dorothy Lewis saying that she welcomed the Christian service because she believed that God saved her family: "I can't go to sleep for thanking Him. I wake up in the morning thanking Him." Another reporter critically quoted Protestant minister William Lawson telling the evacuees, in a government building, that "God hasn't forgotten you, no more than He had forgotten Job."

Some skeptical journalists did not hide what they had seen. Bill Berkowitz of the Inter-Press Service, a critic of conservative organizations, noted: "In light of President Bush's anemic immediate response to the catastrophe, the lack of effective pre-hurricane planning by state and local government, and FEMA's failure to provide timely assistance to the victims, the faith-based community mobilized quickly. Thousands of vigorous and enthusiastic volunteers who were affiliated with a broad assortment of religious groups stepped up to feed the hungry, shelter the homeless, and serve the needy in countless ways."

The usual critics were generally silent, because after Katrina, Christians were the Dirty Harrys of social service in today's America. The 1971 film *Dirty Harry* starred Clint Eastwood as a San Francisco cop hated by the liberal mayor but called upon when the going got rough. In the movie the Eastwood character gained his nickname because he took on the most difficult tasks that the city could offer. "Now you know why they call me 'Dirty Harry,'" he told his partner after heroically saving one person from death. "[I take] every dirty job that comes along."

Action by Christians sometimes produced extraordinary reactions. For example, an atheist writing in the leftist British *Guardian Weekly* commented two weeks after Katrina hit that he had seen how Christians "are the people most likely to take the risks and make the sacrifices involved in helping others. . . . The correlation is so clear that it is impossible to doubt that faith and charity go hand in hand." He ended his article: "It ought to be possible to live a Christian life without being a Christian or, better still, to take Christianity a la carte. Yet men and women who, like me, cannot accept the mysteries and the miracles do not go out with the Salvation Army at night. The only possible conclusion is that faith comes with a packet of moral imperatives that, while they do not condition the attitude of all believers, influence enough of them to make them morally superior to atheists like me. The truth may make us free. But it has not made us as admirable as the average captain in the Salvation Army."

That Katrina prompted such a realization, and many others like it, indicates that some good came of it, just as some good came of calamities in the Roman Empire during the second and third centuries. That's when Tertullian, writing about Christianity, said, "It is our care for the helpless, our practice of loving kindness that brands us in the eyes of many of our opponents. 'Only look,' they say, 'how they love one another.'"

In the fourth century as well, disasters brought not festivals of finger pointing but opportunities to show compassion. Bishops such as Basil of Caesarea urged the rich to offer aid amid famine, and many did. He built the first real hospital; other Christians established *xenodocheia*, homes for foreigners, and *ptocheia*, homes for the poor, at a time when the declining Roman Empire was showing kindness to neither. This became a great tradition, and perhaps it is being reemphasized in the twenty-first century. We'll turn to that question in the next chapter.

Chapter 6

RECOVERY AND RELIGION

After disaster rescue and relief comes recovery, which is not only material but religious and psychological as well. This is more than a theoretical statement: it seems that questions of faith are universal when disaster hits. When the president of Turkey arrived in Erzincan in December 1939 to survey the results of an earthquake that occurred two days previously, killing fifty thousand, an elderly woman wearing a black dress covered with dust ran past security guards and demanded, "President! President! My family is gone! Why? Why?"

President Inonu could have told her that her family died because her husband and son were crushed by sand and rocks they had placed on the roof to provide additional winter insulation, but that wasn't the question she was asking. Those who surveyed the Katrina wreckage also sought for meaning. Veteran relief director Robert Reccord said, "I've been in a lot of disaster relief settings, and I have never seen anyone respond, 'Don't push that religious stuff on me.' When physical trauma and need exist, there is inevitably a deep-seated spiritual need in the heart of people. Nobody puts it there; nobody tries to create it. It's simply there because of the tenuous nature of life."

The highly secularized *Washington Post* recognized at least the psychological difficulties in a December 2005 story headlined "Katrina's Emotional Damage Lingers." The article began with a quotation from a man who remained in New Orleans and said that until Katrina struck, "I'd hardly had a drink in years." He said, "Right after the hurricane hit, I just started drinking. If I stop drinking, the pain becomes so great it's unbearable." The *Post* dramatically described New Orleans residents "walking on deserted streets with glazed eyes. . . . In grocery stores and offices, they inexplicably break into tears." The *Post* noted, "Every disaster has its second wave, the emotional scars that linger after the initial blow."

THE BIBLE AND DISASTER

Rick Warren, author of *The Purpose Driven Life*, also spoke of two needs of disaster victims: "The first perspective is physical—saving and sustaining lives, followed by spiritual—helping people deal with trauma by putting their faith and trust in God, which cannot be taken away." Warren and other Christians saw the Bible as helpful in dealing with such "second wave" comments and problems. The Bible contains numerous references to disasters and their origins, particularly in the prophetic books. For example, Isaiah 10:2 explains that God sends disaster to discipline those who "turn aside the needy from justice and . . . rob the poor of my people of their right, that widows may be their spoil, and that they may make the fatherless their prey!"

Jesus himself gave clear instructions when he critiqued those who were judging the victims of one recent disaster: "Those eighteen on whom the tower in Siloam fell and killed them: do you think that they were worse offenders than all the others who lived in Jerusalem? No, I tell you; but unless you repent, you will all likewise perish" (Luke 13:4). Jesus, it seems, would tell the woman in Erzincan, Turkey, or the staggering residents of

New Orleans that horror did not come to their doors because those who died were worse offenders than others, but as warnings to all.

Another time, Jesus spoke of the opportunity that sad occurrences provide: "He saw a man blind from birth. And his disciples asked him, 'Rabbi, who sinned, this man or his parents, that he was born blind?' Jesus answered, 'It was not that this man sinned, or his parents, but that the works of God might be displayed in him. We must work the works of him who sent me while it is day; night is coming, when no one can work" (John 9:1–4). In essence, we don't know why disasters hit particular people, but we do know that they should push all of us toward doing the works that God commands—which, in the case of widows, orphans, aliens, and those with disabilities, means to exercise compassion.

As chapter 2 showed, press liberals tried to make political capital of Katrina by pointing fingers at the Bush administration. Sadly though, some conservatives did cultural politicking by pointing fingers at New Orleans residents, as if those struck were more sinful than others. Alabama state senator Hank Erwin said that the hurricane hit New Orleans and the Mississippi Gulf Coast because of "gambling, sin and wickedness."

Rev. John Westcott of Ansonia, Connecticut, specified the Mardi Gras "orgy of drunkenness, drug abuse, and sexual promiscuity." Rev. Dwight McKissic of Cornerstone Baptist Church in Arlington, Texas, said, "New Orleans flaunts sin in a way that no other places do."

That finger pointing may make sense if we only look at the destruction of Sodom and see all other disasters as parallel. But the Bible overall speaks, as Jesus did, of generalized sin, and when it points to particular sins is more likely to cite the economic than the sexual. Micah 2:2 prophesied that disaster will come because "they covet fields and seize them . . . they oppress a man and his house, a man and his inheritance." Any city in the United States could be guilty of that. Jeremiah 5:28 has a similar message: "They judge not with justice the cause of the fatherless, to make it prosper, and they do not defend the rights of the needy." In what city anywhere in the world has such robbery and injustice not occurred?

Some mainstream publications could not resist the tendency to depict all Christians as fanatics. On the seventh day of Katrina week, the *Washington*

Post, not resting, headlined one story "Where Most See a Weather System, Some See Divine Retribution." It found a little-known pro-lifer for its lead: "Steve Lefemine, an antiabortion activist in Columbia, South Carolina, was looking at a full-color satellite map of Hurricane Katrina when something in the swirls jumped out at him: the image of an eight-week-old fetus." The *Post* then quoted Lefemine: "God judged New Orleans for the sin of shedding innocent blood through abortion."

The *Post* also found the Web site of a Stan Goodenough, who connected the removal of Jewish settlers from the Gaza Strip with the evacuation of New Orleans residents: "Is this some sort of bizarre coincidence? Not for those who believe in the God of the Bible. . . . What America is about to experience is the lifting of God's hand of protection; the implementation of His judgment on the nation most responsible for endangering the land and people of Israel."

With the *Post* and other publications doing such diligent research, journalists could once again connect American fundamentalists with Muslim extremists. Newspapers quoted al Qaeda's Abu Musab al-Zarqawi: "America has been hit by a divine strike." Jihadist blogs enthused: "Katrina, a soldier sent by God to fight on our side. The soldier Katrina joins us to fight against America." Louis Farrakhan made a press comeback with his exultation: "God is whipping America."

PASTORAL INTERPRETATIONS

Google and LexisNexis searches show that such interpretations of Katrina were rare among American evangelical leaders. The view of Bishop T. D. Jakes of The Potter's House in Dallas was far more common: "I'm not sure that we can say that New Orleans is any more wicked than Paris or Los Angeles or New York or even Dallas. I have learned, in the soon-to-be thirty years that I've been in ministry, to stick to the Scriptures and leave what is in the mind of God to God himself."

Pastor John Piper of Bethlehem Baptist in Minneapolis emphasized God's message to all people, as Jesus teaches in Luke's Gospel concerning the tower of Siloam: "Weep both for the perishing and for ourselves who will soon follow. Whatever judgment has fallen, it is we who deserve it—all of us." Piper then spoke about the "arrogance in our own hearts" to think either that God has nothing to do with disaster or that God is punishing a particular group of sinners lacking in the virtue that finger pointers think they have. He then emphasized the mercy inherent in God's sometimes-inscrutable plan: "You meant evil . . . but God meant it for good" (Gen. 50:20).

Piper spoke of how Christ "stood on the sea and stopped the waves with a single word" (Mark 4:39). Piper said, "Even if nature or Satan unleashed the deadly tidal wave, one word from Jesus would have stopped it. He did not speak it. This means there is design in this suffering. And all His designs are wise and just and good. One of His designs is my repentance. Therefore I will not put God on trial. I am on trial. Only because of Christ will the waves that one day carry me away also bring me safely to His side."

David Crosby, pastor of First Baptist of New Orleans, typified the ministerial emphasis on the opportunity Katrina provided to do the works of God, as Jesus teaches in John's Gospel. Crosby said, "Across the devastated area, believers in the Lord Jesus are prominent in helping strangers dig out of the rubble. This hard and dirty work will plant seeds that will produce a hundredfold for the Kingdom of God. Already people are trusting Christ. They are startled by our concern for them and our willingness to help them out. And the resistance to the gospel of grace in the Lord Jesus is falling away." Cosby prayed "that God will turn this great natural disaster into the greatest spiritual revival in the history of our nation."

Did journalists downplay opinions of representative leaders in favor of those who fit the stereotype of Christians as haters? To answer that question, it's worth checking the December 2004 Barna poll that asked 614 Protestant ministers to name the "most trusted" spokesmen for Christianity. Billy Graham, James Dobson, and Rick Warren finished 1-2-3; Pat Robertson was down on the list, named by only 4 percent of respondents. Graham and Dobson apparently did not speak out about the meaning of the hurricane, but Warren and Robertson did.

An observer from Mars might think that Warren's statements would receive greater press attention both because of his greater following among ministers and because he spent three days visiting disaster victims and telling one and all: "God loves to bring good out of bad. . . . He loves to bring resurrections from crucifixions. . . . This is an opportunity for the Church to be the Church and to show the world what we're for instead of what we're against. . . . God is at work in people who are showing his love in practical ways, feeding, caring, clothing. I've been in churches that are taking people in by the hundreds. It's an amazing thing."

Robertson, meanwhile, did not visit areas hit by Katrina and said little, perhaps remembering the lambasting he received four years earlier for saying the 9/11 disaster was God's punishment of America. His only comments were an odd suggestion on September 1 that John Roberts would receive easier questioning because hurricane news trumped his Supreme Court nomination, and an oblique comparison of abortion to "natural disaster" on September 12.

Reporters desperately seeking fanaticism, though, played up even a toned-down Robertson. Press accounts in the LexisNexis database connected "Pat Robertson" and "Katrina" six times as often (337 times) in the month following the hurricane's landfall as they connected "Rick Warren" and "Katrina" (58 times). LexisNexis had a similar six-to-one ratio concerning two lesser-known Christian leaders, Michael Marcavage (30 citations) and Albert Mohler (5), even though Marcavage heads up a tiny Pennsylvania fringe group called Repent America and Mohler is president of Southern Baptist Theological Seminary, the largest seminary of the largest Protestant denomination in the country.

It's not hard to posit one possible reason for the differential. Marcavage was saying, "God destroyed a wicked city . . . that had its doors wide open to the public celebration of sin. . . . The day Bourbon Street and the French Quarter was flooded was the day that one hundred twenty-five thousand homosexuals were going to be celebrating sin in the streets." (Actually, the French Quarter did not flood, but flooding buried Desire Street Ministries, a great example of Christian ministry to the poor.) Mohler, though, said of Katrina, "We have no right to claim that we know what this storm means." He noted that God rebuked Job's friends who contended that he was being punished for his own misdeeds. Mohler did not fit press stereotypes.

WORLDVIEWS AND DISASTER

"My family is gone! Why? Why?" the Turkish woman asked many years ago. "New Orleans is gone! Why? Why?" others asked last year. The answers varied by worldview. The nonreligious suggested options A or B: either disasters arise merely out of bad luck and are thus totally devoid of meaning, or the proximate reason is personal or organizational fault (and there is no ultimate reason). An immediate media search for perpetrators is the only alternative to admitting that a hurricane's sound and fury is just that, signifying nothing. If journalists do not major in the politics of disaster, they have to admit to the meaninglessness of disaster—few but the bravest existentialists care to admit that.

Religious answers differed. Hindus believe that disaster results from karma, payback for evil committed in previous lives. Karma is individual, not collective, but the cumulative bad karma of half a million individuals could send a hurricane careening toward a city. In that sense New Orleans suffered because New Orleans deserved to suffer. This theology packs a political punch, because attempts to mitigate disaster or bind up the wounds of the sufferers may be counterproductive in the long term, since taking the full brunt of what spiritual forces dish out this time may make for better lives in the next incarnation.

Animistic and polytheistic religions offered another alternative: the residents of New Orleans may have in some way brought down curses on themselves from powerful gods. Perhaps construction irritated the Mississippi river god, and perhaps attempts to construct hurricane-proof buildings upset Aeolus, the god of the winds. These viewpoints also suggest a political response: back off from attempts to mitigate the effects of flooding by engineering, lest we anger the malign children of Mother Nature.

In Christianity, though, disasters result not from chance, karma, or curses, but from God's mysterious providence, which no one ever understands fully. The nineteenth-century preacher Charles Spurgeon put it this way: "Providence is wonderfully intricate. Ah! You want always to see through Providence, do you not? You never will, I assure you. You have not eyes good enough. You want to see what good that affliction was to you;

you must believe it. You want to see how it can bring good to the soul; you may be enabled in a little time, but you cannot see it now; you must believe it. Honor God by trusting him."

Without that type of biblical understanding, journalists with a social conscience are anxious and unable to recognize the quality of God's mercy. In Leo Tolstoy's great short story "What Men Live By," an angel is distressed when twin babies, whose father has been killed in a logging accident, are about to lose their mother as well. "Little children cannot live without father or mother," the angel tells God, and refuses to take the mother's life. Sent to earth helpless and wingless to learn some important lessons, the angel eventually realizes that men, women, and even orphans live not by human or even angelic considerations of necessity but by God's mercy.

Few journalists are angels, but we can see such mercy in our own lifetimes if we look. We report "acts of God" such as hurricanes and hard storms but often ignore the far more numerous acts of God that keep us alive day by day. We read reports of terrible auto accidents, but we never know how many just as horrible were barely averted. We do see international mercies as well, but they quickly tend to be taken for granted. How often do we ponder the amazingly rapid end of the Soviet Union after decades of oppression, or the nonuse of nuclear weapons for over half a century?

Novelist Janie B. Cheaney, writing in *World* with a Christian worldview, emphasized how disaster could even change lives for the better: "Many evangelicals are involved in short-term relief efforts. They are helping displaced people from Louisiana and Mississippi to find shelter and meet basic needs. Other congregations are going further and making long-term commitments to affected individuals and churches. They are giving evacuees the gift of time: time to talk about it, with someone to listen. Time to mend broken connections, find family members, mourn lost friends. Time to consider what to do next. Even time, perhaps, to make a new start in a new community with new friends."

Some of that has happened. The *Washington Post* profiled Bruce Norwood, a forty-eight-year-old who had suffered a minor stroke earlier in 2005 and was a Katrina evacuee to Houston. There he encountered William Finch, a priest who had collected $100,000 from his parishioners at St.

Raphael's Catholic Church in Rockville, Maryland. The funds were to charter a bus to rescue as many evacuees as possible. Norwood stayed at the home of two parishioners for about a month, then moved into his own apartment. He gained a job as a deli sandwich maker at a suburban Maryland supermarket. The *Post* reported, "Norwood is feeling at home in Maryland. His apartment is sparsely furnished, but he has the essentials—a couch, coffee table and bed, all church donations: 'It's a lovely apartment in a very secure neighborhood.'"

Cheaney added: "I'm not naïve about human nature: This massive offering of Christian aid to the poor and tempest-tossed is bringing and will bring disappointments as well as successes. Some evacuees are taking and will take advantage. Some are and will be impossible to discipline. Some are repaying and will repay kindness with retribution over imagined slights. But I keep thinking of how it is for . . . those who were trapped in bad lives, squalid conditions, false ideologies, are blinking in the sunlight. Maybe they will be able to say, 'We went through fire and through water; yet you have brought us out to a place of abundance" (Ps. 66:12).

Some went through fire and water and came out not with depression but with greater faith. The *Washington Post* also profiled a seventy-two-year-old man named Eddie Bourgeois, who had become a widower in June and had to flee New Orleans two months later. He ended up at the D.C. Armory in Washington and faced a future with no obvious security, but to reporters he seemed serene: "Jesus said you're going to have trials and tribulations. I'm not worried. I'm just waiting. I just put it in Jesus's hands." It will be awhile before any long-term improvement in his material circumstances becomes evident, if it does, but his serenity while others screamed had already paid spiritual benefits.

No sane person would wish on New Orleans what it has gone through. But as the months after Katrina slogged by, people remembered that the city was not Eden, and statistics bore that out. According to the U.S. Census Bureau, New Orleans was the fifth-fastest-shrinking city in America. A Milken Institute survey stated it was behind 83 percent of the United States' two hundred largest cities in "creating and sustaining jobs." It featured incompetent government, high taxes, huge numbers of regulations, a poor work ethic, and a lack of dynamism. It was one of America's poorest cities, a place where 1995's welfare reform had born little fruit over the subsequent decade.

So maybe it was not far-fetched for Ms. Cheaney to ask whether, some-day, many of those trapped in New Orleans before Katrina would think of the hurricane as a deliverer that blew them to a better place. Might they actually look back and say, "It was the best thing that ever happened to me"? And, if offering Katrina help might begin a revitalization of many churches as well, another Cheaney question is important: "Could this terrible storm one day cause some church historian to write of American Christians, 'This was their finest hour'?"

Part Three

HOW TO REFORM NATIONAL DISASTER POLICY

When President Bush, stung by accusations of mean-spiritedness during the Katrina disaster, declared the floodgates of federal spending open, press critics guffawed at what compassionate conservatism had become. For example, columnist Jonah Goldberg wrote, "Here's my silver-lining hope this hurricane season: George W. Bush's compassionate conservatism gets wiped out like a taco hut in the path of a Cat. 5 storm."

Wall Street Journal columnist Peggy Noonan, though, protested the misapplication. She noted accurately that compassionate conservatism had meant not action "to avoid criticism, but to make things better." She continued: "It meant an active and engaged interest in poverty and its pathologies. It meant a new way of doing old business, [not] a return to the pork-laden legislation of the 1970s. We did not understand it to mean never vetoing a spending bill. . . . We did not understand it to be a step back toward old ways that were bad ways."

It meant individuals and private organizations taking action, as in this September 6, 2005, Associated Press account from Olivia, Minnesota, that described one of many similar occurrences: "It was a quick trip—nearly two thousand three hundred miles in fifty-two hours—as six buses, a truck and a support vehicle drove from Minnesota to Louisiana and back with supplies for victims of Hurricane Katrina. The caravan delivered ninety to one hundred thousand pounds of food, water, diapers, and hygiene items to Shreveport and Natchitoches. Matt Holland of Olivia teamed with another driver to man one of the buses. He arrived home at 12:30 a.m. and got up five hours later to get back in the bus and bring students to school."

Now that we've examined in parts 1 and 2 what went wrong and what went right in reactions to Katrina, let's assess what's wrong and right with our overall disaster policy. Katrina problems were not just a Cajun occurrence but also the culmination of bad, old ways, and a plea for compassionate and efficient substitutes.

Chapter 7

WELFARE FOR THE RICH AND THE POOR

To put it bluntly, the operative National Response Plan of the Department of Homeland Security is unworkable.

The plan is fifty-three thousand words long, and many of the fifty-three thousand are acronyms, 156 in all and oft-repeated. The plan references APHIS (Animal and Plant Health Inspection Service), CDRG (Catastrophic Disaster Response Group), CERT (Community Emergency Response Team), DEST (Domestic Emergency Support Team), DMORT (Disaster Mortuary Operational Response Team), DTRIM (Domestic Threat Reduction and Incident Managment), EPLO (Emergency Preparedness Liaison Office), and on through the alphabet.

The plan begins grandly by labeling itself "a unified, all-discipline, and all-hazards approach to domestic incident management." It says, "This approach is unique and far reaching in that it, for the first time, eliminates critical seams and ties together a complete spectrum of incident management activities to include the prevention of, preparedness for, response to, and recovery from terrorism, major natural disasters, and other major emergencies."

After Katrina, this talk of eliminating critical seams sounds like a bad joke.

But there's more: "The end result is vastly improved coordination among Federal, State, local, and tribal organizations to help save lives and protect America's communities by increasing the speed, effectiveness, and efficiency of incident management [through] extensive vetting and coordination with Federal, State, local, and tribal agencies, nongovernmental organizations, private-sector entities, and the first-responder and emergency management communities across the country."

Homeland Security tells us to rest easy because the NRP covers "not only the traditional spectrum of man–made and natural hazards—wildland and urban fires, floods, oil spills, hazardous materials releases, transportation accidents, earthquakes, hurricanes, tornadoes, pandemics, and disruptions to the Nation's energy and information technology infrastructure—but also the deadly and devastating terrorist arsenal of chemical, biological, radiological, nuclear, and high-yield explosive weapons."

After all that buildup, the plan that is supposed to keep us safe from everything is disappointing. Much of it has to do with relations among city, state, and federal officials—a vital issue, as Katrina proved—but in these sections the computer-like assurance suddenly disappears and we're left in the realm of judgment calls: "A Governor may request the President to declare a major disaster or emergency if the Governor finds that effective response to the event is beyond the combined response capabilities of the State and affected local governments. . . . The President may grant a major disaster or emergency declaration."

At the end of fifty-three thousand words, the NRP offers no way out of the tangle of local, state, and federal responsibilities that contributed to failure in New Orleans. The plan clarifies one aspect, mistakenly: it establishes the Red Cross as the agency that is supposed to carry out relief tasks comprehensively and efficiently. It does not clarify crucial lines of governmental responsibility but says they are to be negotiated—and when minutes mean lives, negotiation takes too long. Especially when responsibilities are unclear, hurricanes bring with them not only storm surges but also blame surges. If the NRP governs the next disaster, another surge is inevitable.

Perhaps our political leaders could deal with the problem by undertaking the tenth or twentieth bureaucratic reorganization since Washington began paying for disasters in 1950, but success does not seem likely. Federal Circuit Court judge Richard Posner, whose hobby is searching for rationality in precincts where it's hard to find, has it right: he wrote in the *New Republic*, "Our government is incapable not only of dealing with what is merely probable but also of creating rational bureaucratic structures."

Posner observed: "Politicians have limited horizons. Probabilities are relative to the interval over which they are computed, as in my example of the probability of a disastrous flood in New Orleans: the probability was much greater over a period of thirty years than over a period of one year. Few politicians are looking forward to thirty years in office, so they have little incentive to support measures that may be cost-justified only if the horizon of concern is pushed out that far from the present. Their motto is, sufficient unto the day is the evil thereof. Policy myopia is built into democratic politics."

He also noted "rapid turnover, as officials cycle between public sector and private sector jobs. . . . The "revolving door" is most commonly criticized as a form of soft corruption. That is not the serious problem. The serious problem is the lack of continuity in the management of government, and the consequent foreshortening of the planning horizon. An official who spends only two years in a job is unlikely to be worrying about what may happen (but more likely will not happen) decades hence. He will receive no current reward from planning to deal with contingencies, however ominous, that seem to lie in the remote future."

The business executives who moved quickly once Katrina hit may have been better leaders than their governmental counterparts, but they also had a structural advantage. Judge Richard Posner has pointed to a basic problem of "overextension of the federal government." He said, "It is trying to do too much. In the face of formidable challenges to the safety of the nation . . . the government has entangled itself in contentious, emotional . . . matters such as abortion." Less grievous entanglements also cause overextension: one poll, reported by the *American Enterprise* editor Karl Zinsmeister, showed that 57 percent of Americans want public officials to take charge of rescuing household pets after natural disasters.

WELFARE FOR THE RICH

With constituents asking for everything, political leaders and officials often seem incapable of saying no to interest groups that see a federal gravy train and want to climb aboard. The result is welfare for both the rich and the poor. Let's start by looking at payments to the wealthy: those who have gained billions through the National Flood Insurance Program, which encourages building in beach areas so storm-prone that private insurers do not want to tread there.

ABC's John Stossel has displayed the problem vividly: "In 1980 I built a beach house on the edge of the ocean on Long Island. It was an absurd place to build a house. One block down the road was a desert-like wasteland where a dozen houses had eroded away a few years earlier. Still, my eager-for-the-business architect said,' Why not build? If the ocean destroys your house, the government will pay for a new one.' . . . The contractor was right. . . . During a fairly ordinary storm, the ocean knocked down my government-approved pilings and ate my house. . . . Financially I made out just fine. Federal flood insurance paid for the house—and its contents."

North Carolina resident Betty Minchew, whose oceanfront rental house blew away during Hurricane Hugo in 1989, similarly made use of cheap federal flood insurance—first using government money to rebuild her house and then building two other beachfront rental houses in the same hazardous area. She said, "Hugo was good to me. . . . We had a lot of little shacks out here. Hugo got rid of those, and people built nicer, prettier places." When hurricanes are good to people economically, something is awry. One newspaper reported how Minchew rented out for $650 per wedding event or party a "three-bath edifice with columns and a wall of glass," with that wall an invitation to a profitable smash-up.

Periodic press accounts note the pattern. In 2000 USA Today headlined one article "High-risk Life, High Expense to Taxpayers: Federal Disaster

Aid Makes It Feasible to Build in Harm's Way." As always, entitlements started small: "What began as a trickle of aid for people living near the seacoast has turned into a tidal wave of financial support. The government's ever-expanding generosity has created a vicious cycle for taxpayers: By reducing the economic risks of living near the water, Washington has spurred development. So when each new disaster strikes, the cost of federal assistance rises to cover all new private buildings and public facilities."

Liberal newspapers have occasionally reported on this problem because it does have a populist flair: with much oceanfront property personally used by the wealthy or owned for investment purposes—in which case maintenance, mortgage interest, and depreciation are all tax-deductible—these payments are welfare for the rich. Investors now don't mind hurricanes, and Bob Linville, the mayor of one North Carolina beachfront town, reported that he was hoping for a hit: "Next time we have one, I've got a few places I'm going to paint a bull's eye on."

Making the "welfare for the rich" tag even more evident is the federal government's penchant for enabling the rebuilding of structures in risky locations. Once-bitten private insurers are twice shy and would not keep paying for buildings in risky locations, but legislation forces even officials who know better to repeat errors like Wile E. Coyote. Newspapers such as the *Raleigh News & Observer* have criticized repetitive payments, editorializing about how "residents mined taxpayer accounts to rebuild in fragile areas." The same article stated, "Encouraging any policy that continues a cycle of predictable damage and guaranteed repair—all that sounds like the recipe for chronic disaster."

LEADING US INTO TEMPTATION

Just as welfare for the poor brought about multigenerational dependency on government, so welfare for the rich has also birthed a moral hazard: act irresponsibly and the government will still provide a stipend. The analogy to welfare for the poor stands in one other way as well: it's been said with considerable evidence that the way for a poor teenager to avoid the welfare trap is the simple three-part strategy of graduating from high school, avoiding drugs, and not getting pregnant. The rich could also drastically lower their likelihood of relying on cheap federal insurance by following three rules: don't build in a flood plain or on a beach unless you can afford to lose it all; build a very simple beach structure rather than a palace; and if you do build, take advantage of improved (but much more costly) construction advances that lower risk.

The poor, especially during the past decade of welfare reform, have had more incentive to leave the dole than the government-insured rich have had. University of Massachusetts geography and law professor Rutherford Plant writes in *Disasters and Democracy*: "Imagine that you live in a country where police officers give out crisp $100 bills to drivers caught exceeding the speed limit. This country's Automobile Insurance Administration offers subsidized insurance rates, which will not increase regardless of how many accidents you've had. And if you chose not to have insurance, you are still in luck: the (separate) Department of Automobiles promises to help you buy a new car, whether or not your wrecked car was insured."

When George W. Bush became president, his administration, early on, tried to eliminate discounted federal insurance premiums for beachfront vacation, rental, and commercial properties. Some state and local officials in southeastern states acknowledged that it wasn't right for those policyholders, almost always affluent, to pay only a third of what they would without a government discount—but they also reminded Bush officials that these states voted Republican (barely, in Florida's case). When voters like Becky Lenker of Topsail Beach, North Carolina—her house had flooded four times in the previous five years, with federal payoffs following—protested the administration's attempt by stating loudly that President Bush "can stick it in his ear—and I'm a Republican," the White House listened, and then listed.

Repetitive flood insurance losses display the difficulty that officials within a democracy have in saying no. Private insurance companies require significant premium increases on properties at risk or require property owners to take preventive measures as a condition of writing coverage. If no changes occur, these companies cancel policies—but governments rarely have the will to do that.

The result of government flood insurance was evident after Katrina, not in the poor areas of New Orleans, where homeowners rarely purchased flood insurance, despite its low cost, but in the investment beaches along the Mississippi coast. A *Popular Mechanics* writer observed: "It has become a cliché to say that Biloxi, Miss., looks like a bomb hit it. But it's true. The big hotels that line the beach got hammered by the wind/surge/wave combination. In many cases, all that is left on the ground level is steel beams holding up the higher floors. . . . The beachfront properties were devastated, but only a few hundred yards inland, damage was moderate. Maybe there's a lesson there for developers? Apparently not. Compared to New Orleans, where whole neighborhoods remain deserted, Biloxi is crawling with construction teams. Most of them are busy rebuilding hotels right at the water's edge."

Paid off once, shame on the weather or maybe on the builder; paid off twice or even six times, shame on those who write enabling laws and regulations. Some have proposed continuing federal flood insurance but barring construction of homes and hotels on property adjacent to the waves. The Competitive Enterprise Institute, though, offered a simpler proposal: "If the government is concerned about the potential environmental impact of subsidized coastal development, then the government should simply end the subsidies." The Political Economy Research Center also noted that there is no need to restrict property rights when eliminating federal subsidies will do the job.

Those objections make sense for several reasons. The government doesn't buy accident insurance for individuals—nor does it buy it even on condition that an individual will not go skydiving—so why should it in this case? Why should an investment in beachfront property be treated differently than an investment in stock? Stock investments can become worthless, and so can property. The solution is to stop providing federal flood insurance and, instead, offer beachfront property owners three choices. They can pay the market cost of insurance, which would be high; they can go without insurance altogether, in the realization that they need to be able to afford a total loss; or they can sell their property to someone willing to take the first or second choice.

The problem is not restricted to property exposed to wind and wave. Governmental payments for earthquake and fire damage create a similar "moral hazard," by which individuals build and buy properties in risky areas that they would skirt if money for rebuilding came from their own pockets. Welfare for the rich also leads many not to make home improvements that would make them less likely to collapse. Scholar Mary Comerio writes about earthquake preparation, "Despite all the efforts at public education, people are not voluntarily improving their homes and commercial buildings." Nor are they scrambling for more insurance. Instead, Comerio states that most are "repeating what has become the disaster mantra: 'Why pay for insurance? If it's that bad, FEMA will come and write us a check.'"

The upshot: cities pushing for rapid development and consequent tax revenue are more likely to allow or even encourage risky construction when federal bailouts are available for buildings that will literally need to be bailed out. When private insurers believe that building in certain areas is unsafe or actuarially foolish, and therefore refuse to offer policies, the willingness of the federal government to step in encourages people who should have been discouraged and leaves them with a false sense of security.

The Lord's Prayer declares, "Lead us not into temptation," but that's exactly what disaster relief has done for many Americans. Federal disaster relief at one level oozes sympathy for the victims of wind, earthquake, or fire—but the second-order consequences have been severe.

WELFARE FOR THE POOR

Some of the unanswered questions about New Orleans are: Why, forty years after the Great Society began, were one out of four New Orleans residents living below the poverty line, with most of them reliant on government for transportation? Why was New Orleans a failing city, with only tourism keeping it from falling deep into the muck? And why did residents lack both upward and horizontal mobility despite decades of economic support? The Superdome refuge represented a microcosm of forty years of governmental help: the poor had some food and water, a roof over their heads (with panels blown off), and little safety or security.

The painful evacuation gave many residents the opportunity to begin anew and potentially put them in touch with those who could help. One poverty expert—not someone with an academic degree, but a person who had fought her way out of it—made this offer of personal help to a needy evacuee: "I am a black single mom and can house another black single mom and one to two children under two for free for three months. . . . I have been on welfare and put myself through school. In no way have I been through what you have been through, but I can try to help you navigate confusing systems. Just be respectful of the resources that I can provide. . . . No smoking, no drugs, no profanity. . . . Also, limited or no TV. . . . I can help you make it!!!"

Franklin Graham, head of the relief agency Samaritan's Purse and son of the famous evangelist Billy Graham, wrote with fewer exclamation marks but equivalent passion, noting that FEMA was spending $5 billion on temporary housing for Katrina evacuees but that faith-based groups were "struggling to acquire trailers for families ready to move in." He said, "Every trailer that Samaritan's Purse has been able to acquire has been quickly occupied." He was asking "each partner church to commit to taking five trailers that will house hurricane victims—regardless of religious affiliation, race, or creed—for one year. Each church . . . is responsible for providing land to house the trailers in its community. The church must identify a family to occupy each trailer home, maintain the trailer, and assist that family in its transition to permanent housing." Churches would help also with job placement and integration of the family into a new community; after a year, a new family in need could move into the trailer.

Graham's plan differed radically from FEMA's approach of recreating past patterns of economic segregation by housing evacuees in massive trailer parks that, based on previous experience, would quickly devolve into ghettos of despair. World profiled some survivors of Florida's 2004 hurricanes who, a year after the disaster, were still living in a Punta Gorda FEMA camp that had 550 trailers situated eight feet apart on grassless, treeless land. Residents had few expenses because of government largesse but also little income, since job opportunities were rare. The compound was a gated community of sorts—it was surrounded by a tall, chain-link fence—but was still riddled with crime.

The new camps for Katrina evacuees soon had similar problems, as did other FEMA programs: it became apparent that federal disaster payments for housing the poor are as readily abused as welfare payments have been at times. Three months after Katrina, a *Detroit News* headline summarized the results of its investigation: "Evacuees Leave, but U.S. Pays. Taxpayers Pick Up the Tab for Vacant Rooms." FEMA was paying at least $325 per room per week for nine evacuees not staying at one hotel: "FEMA, which has some five thousand seven hundred hotels across the country still housing fifty-three thousand people, has no procedure for checking the accuracy of hotel bills, making the potential for over-billing large."

The *News* tracked one ghost occupant, Anthony Wells, who had returned to New Orleans three weeks before. The hotel manager said FEMA was being charged for another ghost evacuee because he "told the front desk he would return to the hotel from New Orleans at some point. [Others also] have left the hotel for extended periods of time while remaining registered." Another room charged to FEMA housed "two women who declined to provide their names but who confirmed they were from Detroit and that there were no evacuees staying in the room." The hotel may have been deliberately padding the bill, but the manager blamed the evacuees: "Ninety-five percent of the problem is people aren't checking out. . . . These are adults. I'm not going to monitor their comings and goings. If I don't see them in twenty-four hours, I'm not going to check their room."

Assuming that payment for the ghost rooms continued because of confusion rather than deliberate corruption, the manager's point is an excellent one. Its implications may go beyond the particular application he was making: these are adults, and a system where they don't even pay a dollar of their own, and thus have no incentive to make sure they check out of a room, treats them as small children. Just as disaster-related welfare for the rich enables them to build foolishly on sand rather than rock, so welfare for the poor treats them not as adults but as creatures who have no need for anything beyond what homeless shelters refer to as "three hots and a cot."

At the end of 2005, rebellion against how FEMA did business seemed to be breaking out among the agency's employees themselves. Morale had long been a problem. When the Partnership for Public Service in 2003 measured the best places to work in the federal government, FEMA's employees ranked their agency last of twenty-eight government agencies. A 2004 government survey showed only ten of eighty-four FEMA professionals calling the organization "excellent or good." But disputes went public when Scott Wells, FEMA's coordinating official for Louisiana, called the trailer program wasteful and counter to the long-term interests of those displaced.

Senator Collins argued that FEMA should not set up more trailer camps but should give vouchers that could be used for housing anywhere. That ran counter to FEMA's emphasis, often pushed by local politicians, of keeping evacuees close to the evacuated areas. Although Mayor Nagin moved his family to Dallas, he did not want his constituents leaving the city permanently, and constantly advocated their return and rebuilding New Orleans along pre-Katrina lines. That raised a host of political and cultural issues that the next chapter will examine.

Chapter 8

LET'S GET REAL

Three months after Katrina, the *New York Times* reported: "Amid all the arguments over how to rebuild this pummeled city, there is one universally held article of faith here: New Orleans must have a flood protection system strong enough to withstand category five storms, the worst that nature can spawn. It is a rallying cry heard on radio broadcasts and in a front-page editorial in the *Times-Picayune*, in ruined neighborhoods and in corporate boardrooms."

Hmmm . . . in one of the most diverse cities in a diverse America, one universally held article of faith remained. It was an expensive article of faith, costing at least $32 billion of other people's money. It was an article of faith that demanded no change in New Orleans culture but huge technological fixes along the periphery: massive improvements to levees and pumps, sea gates near the Gulf of Mexico, and other transformations based on the experience of The Netherlands, which after a disastrous flood in

1953 began to make improvements that would protect the country against a flood likely to occur only once every ten thousand years.

One counterargument to such U.S. spending is that The Netherlands had no choice: as the name of the country indicates, it's below sea level. The United States, however, is a big country, and many questioned whether it makes sense to rebuild the small part that could readily be underwater once again. Others asked whether even the most expensive protective system could guard against all eventualities, especially since the next storm could come from the west rather than the southeast: Lt. Gen. Carl A. Strock of the Army Corps of Engineers said, "We don't need to be fighting the last war all the time."

Dutch engineers also noted that even a $32 billion expenditure would bring no Dutch-like guarantee of success, because The Netherlands does not experience hurricanes. Furthermore, now that the whole world has seen what a breach in the levees can do, hasn't New Orleans become easy prey for terrorists? Scott A. Angelle, the secretary of Louisiana's Department of Natural Resources, insisted, "We can fix anything that we focus on. We, as a people, and we, as Americans." Given the national need to improve education and health care, and to integrate a new generation of immigrants, how much time and money do Americans want to spend on below-sea-level New Orleans?

Is rebuilding New Orleans what we, as Americans, must do, or would it make us like ancient Romans? In AD 62 when a large earthquake near Mount Vesuvius destroyed Pompeii's water and sewer system, even a bread-and-circuses spender like Emperor Nero wondered whether the city should be rebuilt almost in the shadow of a volcano. But Pompeii residents, loving their location, spent funds on reconstruction—and in AD 79 a Vesuvius eruption buried Pompeii, Herculaneum, and Stabiae under cinders and ash.

Vesuvius erupted again in AD 203, and after that the next big Vesuvius blowout didn't occur until AD 472. Hurricanes brush or hit New Orleans, though, once every four years, with a direct hit every thirteen years: the list includes Brenda, Esther, Hilda, Camille, Bob, Elena, Florence, Andrew, Hermine, Bertha, Isidore, Matthew, and Cindy. With major hits such as

Betsy in 1965 and Katrina in 2005 coming once in a generation, New Orleans rebuilding is a risk that Romans might decline. They may have had more of an understanding of the constraints of the environment than we in the twenty-first century have, since we now spend part of our lives in the virtual reality presented by computers and media.

DODGING REALITY

A tendency to see ourselves as masters of the universe has increased risks in other ways as well. For decades now Congress has made appropriations to build up areas prone to flooding, construct flood walls that force water into narrow channels, and drain wetlands in the center of the country that served as safety valves during periods of heavy rain. That has led to an increasing number of floods: the Mississippi topped flood levels at Davenport, Iowa, five times in the first half of the twentieth century and twenty-four times in the second. Federal officials have since told prospective builders to have no fear for the government is here, ready to pay out where insurance companies fear to tread.

Increasing complexity has moved us further from living simply; the bigger we are, the harder we fall. A loss of electricity would mean nothing in a society reliant on candles for light or ice for keeping food cool. Electricity, cars, phones, computers—all are good to have and use, as long as we are prepared to do without them for short periods of time. Yet most individuals and families have not developed the habit of keeping basic supplies and having alternative means of lighting, heating, or news gathering. Evidently, most people who stayed in New Orleans did not store three days of food and water, nor did they have a battery- or crank-operated radio so as to follow events outside their immediate vantage point.

Meanwhile the population in U.S. coastal areas has increased. In 1960 an average of 187 people lived on each square mile of U.S. coast, excluding Alaska. However, that population density exploded to 275 per square mile in 1995 and is expected to reach about 330 by 2015. Better highways have accompanied population growth, but evacuations in the 1960s were still faster than recent ones. Great population growth has also occurred along fault lines most likely to erupt into devastating earthquakes, and in fire-prone, brushy canyons.

As we refuse to take into account the building risks in some areas, so we refuse to adjust our plans significantly when catastrophes occur. President Bush reacted to the huge cost of Katrina relief by proposing only modest budgetary reductions, $15 billion in fiscal year 2006. The House of Representatives went for only 60 percent of that, and the Senate for virtually none. It's not as if the budget is already slim: Citizens Against Government Waste (CAGW) prepared a reasonable list of six hundred proposals that could save taxpayers $232 billion in fiscal 2006. Reduction of highway pork alone—$223 million for the "Bridge to Nowhere" (aka the Gravina Island bridge), for example, and $231 million for "Don Young's Way," formerly known as the Knik Arm Bridge, etc.—could save $24 billion.

CAGW, keeping in mind that the Constitution charges the federal government with promoting the general welfare, also proposed killing special-interest appropriations such as those for Alaskan Whaling and Sea Otter commissions, for West Virginia multiflora rose control, and for a bear DNA sampling study in Montana. CAGW had little success, and that's been the pattern over the years: overall, emergency appropriation bills lead to even more rather than less non-disaster-related spending, because the expenditures have to fall within House and Senate budget caps. That's why disaster appropriations in 2003 included funds to establish new centers for the treatment of autism and to recruit more minority dentists. Katrina relief legislation included appropriations for alligator farms and a sugar-cane research laboratory.

Politicians sometimes benefit from disasters because they can do favors and reel in contributions. Bidding wars for political contributors have risen each year like financial tsunamis, even (or especially) when it comes to predictable problems such as beach erosion. Duke University geologist Orrin Pilkey has noted that the cost of beach replacement averages $16,000 a year for a hundred-foot lot, and those who own such lots rarely have problems making $1,000 political contributions. Federal agency heads also may be like ambitious generals who yearn for war: disaster brings their offices more money, employees, interesting travel, and publicity, all with the sense of helping those in need.

EVACUEES AS POLITICAL PAWNS

Politics also played a large role in the question of how to house evacuees whose New Orleans homes had been destroyed. Some Louisiana political leaders, largely Democratic, vociferously opposed plans to resettle storm victims in apartments within host communities across the country, worrying that they would never come back. The problem for the politicos was that few apartments were available in Louisiana. Most were in other states, including perhaps three hundred thousand in Texas. Refugee Council USA—made up of nine U.S. resettlement agencies that from 1975 to 2005 integrated 2.5 million refugees from around the world into American life—contended that Katrina victims should be encouraged not to put their lives on hold but to push for new jobs and new homes in new cities. New Orleans leaders feared exactly that.

In fall 2005 it made great financial sense to encourage people to move into apartments costing $700 per month rather than keeping them in hotels at a cost of $1,800 per room for the same period. Jim Arbury of the National Multi Housing Council, a group of building owners and managers, asked about FEMA: "What are these guys doing? All of this housing is available now." FEMA, in consultation with Louisiana officials immediately after Katrina, agreed to place evacuees in temporary housing, as often as possible within the state. Officials quickly spent $1.5 billion on recreational vehicles and mobile homes: the idea was that evacuees would move from hotel rooms into other temporary housing, thus preserving them for a return to New Orleans.

The embrace of politics over people was too obvious. Just as criticism of the Red Cross became bipartisan following Katrina, criticism of FEMA's housing plans became bi-ideological. Ronald Utt, a senior fellow at the conservative Heritage Foundation, fumed that the reason for FEMA's housing plan was "not incompetence." He said, "This is willful." Bruce Katz, a vice president of the liberal Brookings Institution, said, "We could have thousands, if not tens of thousands of families, in stable permanent housing right now. And we would not have to turn to these costly measures, like hotels, motels and cruise ships." Others paid less attention to economics but opposed the creation of more dysfunctional FEMAvilles, potentially the Hoovervilles of the twenty-first century.

To their credit, Senator Harry Reid and Rep. Nancy Pelosi, the Democratic leaders in Congress, did not go along with the wishes of their New Orleans partymates. Senator Paul S. Sarbanes (D-MD) pushed a plan through the Senate to provide $3.5 billion in housing vouchers to 350,000 Katrina-displaced families. FEMA, under pressure, scaled back plans to build new slums and embraced an alternative proposal: housing vouchers that could give the evacuees a choice while making use of existing housing stock. Late in the year, FEMA began handing out $2,358 vouchers for three months so that families in shelters or hotels could rent apartments.

AN AWOL PRESS

Journalists could have been an immense help by exposing political rip-offs, but instead, many in 2005 rapped about global warming. A LexisNexis search shows the publication of 1,898 pieces with the words "Katrina" and "global warming" during September, with most assuming that the number and intensity of hurricanes were increasing, and many connecting that to global warming. Ross Gelbspan wrote in the *Boston Globe* that the hurricane was "nicknamed Katrina by the National Weather Service, [but] its real name was global warming." Robert F. Kennedy Jr. wrote on the *Huffingtonpost* Web site, "Katrina is giving our nation a glimpse of the climate chaos we are bequeathing our children."

"CNN-ization" makes it seem that the number of hurricanes has increased, but that is an illusion created by the increased coastal population and the vastly increased availability of news about disaster. The National Hurricane Center's listing of hurricanes by category and decade shows that the worst hurricane decade of the past hundred years was the

1940s, with an average of ten category 3 (or higher) hurricanes per year and an average of twenty-four per year in all. The 1930s and 1950s came in a close second and third. The 1960s through the 1990s brought a relative lull, but now we seem to be in a midcentury-like bulge. This is no surprise: scientists have monitored this multidecadal cycle for nearly 150 years, with the incidence of hurricanes being dependent on periodically changing ocean circulation patterns.

The increased recent incidence, though, is startling those who don't know much about meteorological history. Only one of the 1,898 Katrina/global warming articles in September quoted William M. Gray, the head of Colorado State University's Tropical Meteorology Project. He emphasized the cyclical incidence of hurricanes, saying, "There is no reasonable scientific way" that "global warming" would lead to hurricane intensification. Nor did any of the 1,898 articles note the conclusion of the United Nations Environment Programme of the World Meteorological Organization that "the peak strength of the strongest hurricanes has not changed, and the mean maximum intensity of all hurricanes has decreased."

As global warming stories proliferated, journalists tended to ignore a real environmental story growing out of the research of University of Florida professor Daniel Canfield, an expert on flood control and the founder of Lakewatch, an environmental monitoring organization. Although wetlands in general are important in absorbing moisture and reducing the need to build levees ever higher, some lakes in crucial areas present a different picture. Canfield, citing evidence from the 1928 hurricane that sent a killing wall of water across Florida, argues that the draining down of Lake Okeechobee is crucial to prevent a storm surge following a Florida hurricane that could kill thousands. He also contends that it's crucial to remove weeds from canals so they won't clog up pumps during storm flows, and to continue to channel the Kissimmee River.

Powerful environmentalist forces, though, are fighting to preserve Okeechobee as is and to leave the aquatic weeds alone. They are increasing the possibility that Florida will be the next New Orleans. Canfield noted, "While Florida is above sea level, it is bowl-shaped, and a thirty-foot wave could travel all the way across the peninsula, creating just as much damage as Katrina."

The difficulty of correcting Katrina misreporting becomes clearer when we realize it was not an anomaly. Ideological or ratings-driven journalists are getting other stories wrong and have made the same mistakes before. University of California professor Mary Comerio, in *Disaster Hits Home* (University of California Press, 1998), offered history but also prophecy: "Disasters have become big-time news, filling living rooms with images of nature at its most dramatic [and] a relentless stream of images of victims in shock and tears. Then, when the pathos of human suffering becomes stale, reporters begin interviewing victims who demand assistance and blame the government for not helping them fast enough."

This disastrous style of reporting has long-term consequences: politicians make decisions on recovery aid and funding without understanding the extent of the damage and the real condition of housing in the area. Comerio noted: "The constant broadcasting and updating of disaster footage intensified the politicization of disasters light-years beyond the ordinary dimensions of pork-barreling. . . . For every unchallenged tirade against the federal government for failure to deliver more services, the federal agencies tried to improve their tattered images by offering more dollars and more services than ever before."

NEEDED: JOURNALISTIC SKEPTICISM

Only rarely have journalists ever gone beyond sensationalism to take a gimlet-eyed view of federal overspending. In 1998 when Bill Clinton overdid it by declaring Massachusetts a "major disaster" following major rainfall in the Boston area, even the front page of the liberal *Boston Globe* looked up in wonder: "Be careful. It's a disaster out there. That's the word from President Clinton, [who declared] the city of Boston and all of Suffolk, Middlesex, Essex, Bristol, and Norfolk counties a national disaster area. . . . Many people expressed surprise at the disaster declaration with its dark connotations of ravage and ruin. No one wanted to return any federal tax dollars, but some wondered at the ease with which the president can bestow federal funds on even a not-quite-reeling community."

The next chapter makes some public policy proposals that could help us prepare for the next disaster and reduce some of the problems when it arises. Little will change, though, as long as reporters act in the ways described in chapter 2: hyping tragedies, cheering additional spending proposals, and jeering at those who do not promise instant relief. Most are part of the problem, pushing politicians to turn ostentatious empathy into an art form, and propelling them to make promises as a way of showing that they feel constituents' pain. By the time the cameras leave, the list of promises is so long that it becomes hard to separate those who truly need help from those who are helping themselves to a windfall.

Journalists could do enormous good by showing how federal disaster assistance has enabled development in high-risk areas and decreased the incentive for individuals and communities to take their own defensive measures. They could expose pork expenditures and probe federal payments for foreseeable difficulties such as high water, wind, and erosion on the coast, or fires on brushy hillsides. They could ask why predictably heavy snowfalls during northern winters should become federal cases. They could also encourage local programs to mitigate hazards. For example, the city of Berkeley, California, allows residents to keep 50 percent of the real estate transfer tax if they seismically upgrade their homes. Over a three-year period, owners upgraded three thousand homes.

The journalistic list of ethical behavior before, during, and after disasters should be simple: be accurate in depicting threats. Wake up those sleeping late, but don't make so much noise all night long that no one can get needed rest. When disaster strikes, concentrate on reporting, not pontificating. Afterward point out the good that is being done and don't cast blame until the evidence is in. Emphasize what's most helpful for families, not for political careers.

Chapter 9

NEW ROLES FOR MAJOR PLAYERS

Wal-Mart CEO Lee Scott, shortly after Katrina hit, offered a radical suggestion: "Instead of having to re-create everything every time, we should ask, 'How do we use the natural infrastructure that exists in American retail?'" In other words, when FEMA is slow and Wal-Mart, Home Depot, FedEx and others are speedy, why not see whether they could take a leading role?

Franklin Graham offered an even more radical idea: let churches and other religious organizations "be major players." He said, "Entrust some of these billions of dollars into their hands. It makes good practical and economic sense for FEMA to get out of the trailer business and look to tap into the efficient response and resources of local churches instead. . . . Let the government do what it does best, and let non-governmental organizations and churches do the rest. The results will be more effective and much less expensive."

These suggestions made sense but also set off alarm bells. Sure, since companies and religious groups had done well, why not move away from seeing disaster relief as a governmental (and primarily federal) task? Why not provide for the common defense with military forces but promote the general welfare by encouraging religious groups and businesses to do all they can in keeping with their callings?

And yet, when anyone—and particularly an evangelist—speaks about putting "billions of dollars" into the hands of religious groups, concerns about tampering with the "separation of church and state" immediately arise. In a parallel way, when a corporate CEO speaks about business taking on some of what have been seen as the social functions of government, some conservatives worry about "social responsibility" cutting into stockholders' profits, and some liberals fear that the dark night of fascism will descend.

In this chapter, we'll put aside fears and look at what the various groups can do best. We've already looked at the role of religious groups, and we'll come back to them in part 4, so let's look first at what we might expect business to do in future disasters. Then we'll examine local government, the military, and what is often the forgotten actor: the individual.

MAXIMIZING CORPORATE HELP

Companies become strong not through the power of love, nor the power of law—unless there is governmental corruption—but through the power of exchange. The record of governmental failure and religious group success in Katrina relief showed the limitations of law and the strength of love. The reliability of Wal-Mart, Home Depot, FedEx, and others showed the usefulness of exchange. Companies may temporarily act in charitable ways, but trying to turn businesses into humanitarian agencies as such, powered by love, will not work. Businesses are out to make money, and that focus is what trains corporate managers to be precise in their analysis.

To put it another way, churches can act in economically nonrational (although not irrational) ways because their goal is to put Christ first.

Government officials can put forth edicts because they operate on the basis of law and power. (When citizens see government as incompetent, as many did in New Orleans, leaders lose support.) But if Wal-Mart tried to be a church, it would fail; and if it had to push its way through a paper jungle filled with the nebulous goals of well-meaning individuals, it soon would be as efficient as FEMA.

Business typically responds better than government in crisis situations because successful executives are used to taking risks and being the first to produce new products; government officials tend to wait for a broad consensus to emerge. Companies tend to emphasize specific results rather than vague ideas of social welfare. They also tend to offer powerful incentives for success and punishments for failure that government jobs with their greater security rarely match. It's not that private-sector people are more virtuous than government staffers, but they commonly have a results-oriented focus: tunnel vision is enormously helpful when we are in a tunnel.

One way to improve disaster relief, then, is to find ways for major companies to serve greater humanitarian purposes without breaking their business charters. Socially responsible companies do not live for short-term killings, but they need to act in ways that provide long-term benefits to stockholders. So here's a suggestion: give companies the opportunity to engage in relief operations that might not be profitable by giving them something in return—exemptions from capital gains and dividend taxes. Shareholders would gain value, and the postdisaster needy would gain more efficient relief than they would otherwise receive—at a cost to the U.S. treasury that could be more than made up by lowered governmental relief costs.

Many practical details would have to be worked out, but the essential concept is that companies that demonstrated their effectiveness during Katrina or subsequent disasters would be eligible for certification as disaster responders. Expectations of company performance during a subsequent disaster would vary by industry—shipping, pharmaceuticals, general merchandise, etc.—but the basic requirement would be devotion of a certain percentage of actual or potential corporate income to disaster-related services.

TWO CHEERS FOR PRICE INCREASES

A second way to bring more goods quickly to needy people is to rethink the whole concept of what the person who delivers goods in an emergency should be paid. After all, in times of disaster goods are always rationed, generally in one of three ways: the needy pay in time (long lines), in money (increased costs for goods), or in hunger or sickness (doing without what's needed). Since a goal in time of disaster is to have supplies rapidly flowing into a distressed area, the way to maximize flow is to give distributors extra rewards for their extra efforts. When extra rewards are banned, the likely result is a shortage, or at least longer lines.

Laws forbidding price increases during and following disasters seem moral: why should the seller take advantage of the misfortunes of the buyer by raising the price of product at a time when the buyer's income is dropping? The experience after Hurricane Andrew in 1992 blasts some reality into this abstraction. Since Florida laws did not allow those with stocks of generators to raise prices in line with what the highest bidders would pay, hardware store owners sold the machines to friends instead of to grocery stores that would have been happy to pay more. The powerless stores remained closed, as did other businesses, and needy people went without. If postdisaster market prices had been allowed, generator sellers would have been happy; the businesses that paid more for them would have been happy because they could make up that cost by opening their doors and selling goods; and consumers would have been happy to be able to buy what they wanted.

In September 2005 the *Los Angeles Times* profiled Paul Clark, who showed up in reeling Gulfport, Mississippi, on Friday of Katrina week with a trailer load of generators; he has done the same after other hurricanes and tornadoes. When generator sales faltered, he returned to Florida to bring back used RVs to sell or rent, providing a place to stay for those who would otherwise be homeless. P. J. Huffstutter's story lead was "Paul Clark makes money off misery." But would misery have decreased if he had not shown up? Let's think the worst of Clark and assume he's greedy: greed may be bad for his soul but not bad for those in need, because greed would lead him to rush to get his products to potential customers.

Huffstutter reported that Clark sold more than one thousand generators during the week after he arrived, at prices ranging from $450 to $1,950. It turned out that his prices were in line with those of Home Depot. But what if they were more expensive? Many stores were closed and stocks were running low: "Lines often stretch out the door; residents may wait for hours in the sun, only to walk away empty-handed. So it can be a relief to come across a stranger who has what you need in the back of his pickup—and can sell it on the spot." Other newspapers reported that Clark sold his generators by a huge sign proclaiming Power to the People, and quoted him as saying, "We were definitely the heroes coming into town."

After Katrina it was uncommon to see a doubling or tripling of the price for items such as generators, for two reasons. First, as Huffstutter found, "Vendors trying to take too much advantage found out quickly that residents were too savvy to bite." He described one highly marked-up generator not making sales and the seller realizing, "I might have to cut my price." That's because the chance to make a profit attracts many sellers. Second, most of the sellers are not thieves, and there is honor among them. One disaster-chaser, Penny Musbek, said, "You have to keep some morals. How can you live with yourself if you're gouging people who have lost so much already?"

The bottom line is that it takes a bottom line to enlist entrepreneurs. The opportunity to make a profit also gives retailers incentive to spend high on transportation costs, either by driving all night themselves or paying extra to have shipping companies fly or drive in special deliveries. Regular prices depend on regular circumstances; why shouldn't abnormal prices accompany abnormal situations? Food shipments to starving people are different, but most of those deciding whether to buy a generator on the Gulf Coast in September do have a choice, since they can go without power for a time. The choice is not between life and death, but between convenience and inconvenience.

Some politicians, though, care little for logic. Many try to make hay when the sun doesn't shine, attempting to win votes during and after a disaster by complaining about prices. Following Katrina, Mississippi attorney general Jim Hood raged about gasoline price increases and said, "I'm going to send some people to the penitentiary before this is over." House Democratic leader

Nancy Pelosi opined, "The price at the pump is becoming oppressive. . . . Something must be done about this." GOP senator Trent Lott, tugged in two directions by Republican ideology and voter servicing, announced that explanation of the economic principles and facts "ain't good enough." He said, "We at least need to empathize. . . . And make it look like we care."

House Democratic Caucus chairman Robert Menendez said that the Bush administration lacked "sensitivity" on the issue, perhaps "because we have two oilmen in the White House." He may have been right, because the two oilmen probably did know something about the gasoline business. Most station owners pay the daily wholesale price for their gas; so to maintain profit margins, they have to raise prices as soon as wholesale prices rise. When the Florida attorney general ran down complaints about gas "price gouging," he found that 95 percent of retailers were responding to the rise of their wholesale costs.

"We view this as a temporary disruption," White House spokesman Scott McClellan said, and he was right. Wholesale prices soon declined, and prices at the pump followed. Nevertheless, a Gallup poll conducted one week after the hurricane showed 79 percent of respondents saying gasoline sellers were taking advantage of Katrina to charge unfair prices.

REINVIGORATING LOCAL GOVERNMENT

Some New Orleans officials responded disastrously to the Katrina catastrophe, and some observers have cited that as evidence that locals are likely to act as yokels during emergencies. The mayors of Gulfport, Biloxi, and other cities, though, came through. Several weeks later when Hurricane Rita was bearing down on Texas, a quick response in Beaumont showed what local governments do best. Beaumont mayor Guy Goodson was driving past the port area and thinking about how to protect city vehicles vital for recovery. He glanced at the U.S. Navy ships in port, had a thought, and within an hour had arranged with two navy captains to load Beaumont's fire trucks, ambulances, bulldozers, and other vehicles, two hundred in all, aboard their massive cargo ships.

An official sitting in Washington would not have seen and seized the opportunity, but proximity is powerful. Local and state authorities know the local situation and have an intimate familiarity with local conditions, which allows better improvisation. Reliance on the feds creates not only immediate problems but also long-term ones, because local and state muscles can readily atrophy. Disasters that close-at-hand leaders could have handled in past years seem beyond their capacity.

The prospect of federal expenditures can create a disincentive for local and state governments to do the work themselves, and even a fiduciary responsibility to local taxpayers not to be prepared: why spend on equipment if the feds will provide it? As Rutherford Platt writes in *Disasters and Democracy* (Island Press, 1999), "The 'moral hazard' thus becomes a self-fulfilling prophecy—it becomes good politics for states and local governments to neglect their own disaster response capabilities in order to make it easier to qualify for a presidential declaration."

The wandering attention of the Orleans Levee District board noted in chapter 1 may have been due partly to ineptitude and boredom, but partly due to this moral hazard. The Army Corps of Engineers regularly warned local officials that many levees were sinking into soft soil, and that floodgate problems also were creating a levee system that was unsafe at any wind speed above that of a category 1 hurricane. Orleans Levee District officials, and their counterparts in other districts, generally responded by persuading the Louisiana congressional delegation to lobby for more federal funding.

Are local and state governments hopelessly inadequate to deal with disasters? If we assume they are and begin viewing Washington officials as first responders, any chance of reviving local control will disappear. The way to start is to insist that the federal government not pay more than 75 percent of relief costs—that's what the still-operative legislation says, but presidents have the option to raise the federal share beyond that, and few have had the power to resist doing what makes them appear warmhearted.

While emphasizing small government, it's also vital to see that the smallest government is not always the answer: U.S. Senate committee hearings late in 2005 showed how tiny levee districts in Louisiana created a hodgepodge of completing claims and opportunities to avoid responsibility.

Local politicians under fire agreed in December 2005 to make changes: the Orleans Levee District Board agreed to place its real estate holdings and marinas under a separate authority, and Louisiana legislators pledged to take action. The larger part of the cure, though, goes beyond legislation: local officials need to look in the mirror and dislike the beaten-down cur they see. We all need to recognize that we are becoming a country of dependent whiners and need to fight that tendency.

Localities that decided to take charge, post-Katrina, reaped benefits. At the end of 2005, *New York Times* reported on the difference between federal inefficiency and local efficiency in two nearby cities: "There are many reasons for the difference between the lack of progress in Pascagoula and the quick cleanup in the Biloxi area. But officials here point fingers at what they consider the No. 1 culprit: the federal government." Where local government was in charge, the work was going faster and at a much lower price. "Something is very wrong here," said Frank Leach, a Jackson County supervisor. "Our federal government is paying an extraordinary amount of money for services that are not being performed adequately."

The *Times*, usually a fan of expansive federal government, found a similar contrast in Louisiana. Reasons for the delay included the complexity of federal contracts; one 192-page contract with a private company included a section on the type of office paper the company would use. Federal officials "repeatedly gave new demands, such as satellite-based measurements on the location of each house, before large-scale clearing could start." Manly Barton, president of the Jackson County Board of Supervisors, said, "There was just so much bureaucracy, so many levels of approvals, that nobody seemed to be able to make a decision and get things done."

Benny Rousselle, president of Plaquemines Parish in Louisiana, noted that even when a house was about to collapse and its owner had approved demolition, the federal government required rigorous structural, historical, and environmental evaluations of the property: "There are so many monitors, so much overhead, it is really slowing this down." Private contractors spent their money on cleanup itself, but the federal government "had nearly eight hundred employees supervising cleanup and has paid as many as three hundred inspectors a rate of $55.79 an hour to monitor the work by the private contractors."

ARMED FORCES DISCIPLINE

Military organizational strength was so impressive in the aftermath of Hurricane Katrina that President Bush wondered out loud about the Department of Defense becoming "the lead agency in coordinating and leading the response effort" after a massive disaster. He noted that the armed forces could handle "massive logistical operations on a moment's notice." Senator John Warner (R-VA) wondered if Congress should reconsider the Posse Comitatus Act of 1878, which keeps a president from using troops to preserve domestic tranquility unless a state's governor officially requests help.

We should proceed cautiously for three reasons. First, we need to avoid giving the military responsibilities for which it is not suited. Bill Leighty, the Virginia governor's chief of staff, spent two weeks in Louisiana helping manage the state response to Katrina. He came away exasperated by FEMA, saying, "But when you tell the 82nd Airborne, 'Secure New Orleans,' they come in and they know exactly what to do and it gets done." Yes, but if the 82nd Airborne had been assigned FEMA's task of tiptoeing through local, state, and federal bureaucracies, it would not have been effective. Armed forces know how to secure a city, but governing a city is different.

Second, it's vital to preserve the armed forces for what they do best. Relief projects that stretch on for months are different in character from emergency help, intensively proffered over a few days, that leaves troops available for deployment elsewhere the following week. Many of today's governmental tasks could be privatized, but the federal government cannot, constitutionally or realistically, outsource the defense of the United States. The question always needs to be posed: will this use of the armed forces impair their readiness for quick military deployment?

A third concern seems overwrought now, but it would be arrogant to say that a military dictator could never emerge in the United States. The late theologian Francis Schaeffer noted three decades ago, in *How Should We Then Live?* (Crossway Books, 1976) that the pressure of dealing with terrorism and other threats might lead Americans to yearn for authoritarian government. Benjamin Franklin's response to a question about what kind of government the Constitution had established is still significant: "A republic, if you can keep it."

Can the armed forces be used in designated ways without giving away state and local control or risking political liberty? Can they be used without assigning them to tasks they aren't qualified to do and risking their unavailability for tasks for which they are? Yes, but the key is defining functions in categories as in part 2: rescue, relief, recovery, and religion. Military forces should be used in short-term rescue operations but rarely in relief, and definitely not in recovery or religion. The relief exceptions might come at times when a disaster has occurred in a place where needed military equipment is available and the civilian equivalent is not, and where relief helps those in need and also serves national security objectives.

The armed forces in New Orleans specialized in rescue, appropriately. Military groups had to arrive with weapons locked and loaded because of misreporting of civic unrest and because many city police went AWOL, but such police use should be avoided. Probably the best example of when to use the armed forces in relief operations comes from Pakistan: the October 2005 earthquake killed seventy-three thousand in mountainous terrain, creating heartrending scenes such as that of two hundred boys and girls buried in the rubble of a school building next to their textbooks. With roads made impassable by landslides, U.S. tandem-rotor, heavy-lift Chinook helicopters were the only vehicles that could reach and supply cut-off villages.

The choppers flew over twenty-five hundred sorties and delivered nearly six thousand tons of aid, including food, shelter material, blankets, medicine, and the equipment needed to set up the only fully functioning hospital in the region. MASH doctors and nurses treated nine thousand patients and performed 350 major surgeries, saving lives and winning the United States high regard in an area where it had been detested. The medical work would not be needed in the United States, where numerous physicians and staffers typically volunteer their services after disasters, but the use of specialized equipment and military training often would be, as it was during Katrina rescue operations.

The humanitarian effort turned out to be an investment in American security as well as Pakistani welfare. Late in 2005 an opinion poll conducted by ACNielsen/Pakistan showed the popularity of the United States increasing and that of al Qaeda plummeting. If radical Muslims were to gain control of a nuclear-armed Pakistan, the axis of evil would expand in the most dangerous way yet, so America's $500 million expenditure saved Pakistani lives and potentially American ones.

INDIVIDUAL PREPARATION

Since relief, like charity, begins in the home, we should also look at what individuals and families can do. Many who suffered through Convention Center misery were there not because their homes were flooded but because they were foodless: had these individuals merely kept a few days of supplies at home, they could have rested while others fretted. Similarly, many who evacuated by car and found themselves in multihour traffic jams had not brought with them grab-and-go backpacks with food, water, medicines, personal care products, and cash.

Ironically New Orleans officials had tried to emphasize individual preparedness by producing a thirty-minute video, scheduled to be televised in September 2005 and also mailed to homes. The *Los Angeles Times* reported two weeks after Katrina hit that seventy thousand copies of the video were sitting on shelves in Los Angeles awaiting a shipping eastward that now would never come. The central message of the video was "Don't wait for the city, don't wait for the state, and don't wait for the Red Cross."

Whether reminded by a video or not, heads of households should think through the disasters most likely (or least unlikely) to occur in their communities: floods, hurricanes, earthquakes, tornadoes, fires, chemical spills, and so forth. They can then list what they and their families would need to survive for a week without outside aid: water, food, shelter, communications, and medicines, for example. Help is likely to arrive in a week's time, unless a nationwide event like a pandemic (see chapter 17) occurs, in which case longer times of self-provision may be necessary.

So let's take a deliberate break from macropolicy issues and look at the micro, the often-overlooked basics. If every household were to make preparations in accordance with the following needs, many disasters would not be as calamitous:

- The average person should drink at least two quarts of water or other liquids per day. An additional gallon per day is typically used for washing, food preparation, and washing clothes and dishes. The best way to store large quantities is in fifty-five-gallon drums, which can be cleaned of bacteria by the addition of ten teaspoons of scent-free bleach. Other water can be stored in two-liter soda bottles, with freshening by four drops of bleach. Water from clean bathtubs and hot water heaters is also usable.

- Wise people stockpile food; fools rush to supermarkets when a crisis occurs and shelves may be empty. Most people can easily add to their regular shopping food that stores well, especially if kept in a cool, dark place. Canned meats and vegetables, protein or fruit bars, dry cereal or granola, peanut butter, nuts, dried fruit, crackers, and canned juices require no refrigeration and little preparation. Those with camp stoves or other nonelectric means of boiling water should add rice, beans, and pasta, kept in a rotation system so that new purchases are put at the back.

- Health supplies should include not only prescription medicines and basics like vitamins and aspirin, ibuprofen, or Tylenol but also moist towelettes, cleansing agents such as isopropyl alcohol and hydrogen peroxide, antibiotic ointment, antiseptic, cotton balls, scissors, tweezers, needles, bandages, thermometers, medicine droppers, tongue depressor blades, antidiarrhea medication, antacids, laxatives, syrup of ipecac, burn ointment, and various sizes of sterile gauze pads, bandages, and dressings.

- Other useful items include a Bible and other books, a supply of cash, extra pairs of prescription glasses or contact lenses, matches, paper towels and plates, toilet paper and garbage bags, plastic utensils, pens and paper, materials to amuse or keep children busy, and a battery-operated radio with a large supply of batteries. The very young will need diapers and perhaps formula. The old may need extra hearing aid or wheelchair batteries; people dependent on dialysis or other life-sustaining treatments need to know the location of all facilities in the area.

- Hurricanes and earthquakes often knock out power sources, so provision for light, heat, and cooking is still important. Lanterns, flashlights, and matches; warm clothing and blankets; and outdoor grills or camping stoves with a supply of propane, are all useful. Residents should know how to turn off gas and electricity to help prevent gas leaks and fires. Those who want to stay in or return to their homes also have to be prepared for what disaster may have wrought. Returnees need to remember to sniff for gas leaks and inspect homes using flashlights, rather than lighting matches or candles.

This list is obviously not comprehensive, but it suggests the need for some planning. Planning is also important for the selection of family rendezvous sites, escape routes, and out-of-state contact persons—for times when communications go down and confusion goes up.

We all need to understand that paperocracy cannot protect us. Alexis de Tocqueville, in his wonderful 1830s book *Democracy in America*, warned of "a new soft despotism" that could arise in America, in which citizens might slowly submit to "an immense, protective power which is alone responsible for securing their enjoyment and watching over their fate." He said, "That power is absolute, thoughtful of detail, orderly, provident, and gentle. It would resemble parental authority if, father-like, it tried to prepare its charges for a man's life, but on the contrary, it only tries to keep them in perpetual childhood. . . . It provides for their security, foresees and supplies their necessities, facilitates their pleasures, manages their principal concerns, directs their industry."

Tocqueville also wrote about what could happen when government "covers the surface of society with a network of small complicated rules, minute and uniform, through which the most original minds and the most energetic characters cannot penetrate, to rise above the crowd." He continued: "The will of man is not shattered, but softened, bent, and guided; men are seldom forced by it to act, but they are constantly restrained from acting. Such a power does not destroy, but it prevents existence; it does not tyrannize, but it compresses, enervates, extinguishes, and stupefies a people, until each nation is reduced to nothing better than a flock of timid and industrious animals, of which the government is the shepherd."

Part Four

THE ROLE OF FAITH-BASED ORGANIZATIONS

The concept is clear. President Bush said, "Because they are closer to the people they serve, our faith-based and community organizations deliver better results than government. And they have a human touch: when a person in need knocks on the door of a faith-based or community organization, he or she is welcomed as a brother or a sister." Franklin Graham noted, "Pastors usually know their community better than government officials do. . . . While the government talks about systems and infrastructure problems, faith-based organizations are able to provide immediate assistance thanks to established relationships with churches on the ground."

The practice is difficult. Following Katrina, Senator Jeff Sessions (R-AL) said it made pragmatic sense to use religious charities to help his state recover: "There's no way the federal government can maintain on its payroll enough people to immediately respond to every single problem. FEMA will never be large enough to fully deal with a hurricane of this size, and we wouldn't want them to." He was right, but how can the effective faith-based groups expand their reach, and can they do so without losing their effectiveness? Developing more productive relations between church and state requires both government and churches to examine their purposes and roles.

The experience does not fit within clear organization charts. One September 7, 2005, Associated Press story from Memphis showed the consternation with which officials, almost everywhere, greet spontaneity: "More than twenty faith-based groups and others have been distributing aid and offering housing without consulting the Memphis Shelby County Emergency Management Agency or American Red Cross, officials said. . . . 'I think some people have gotten upset with me because I'm pushing that they should go through the official process,' EMA director Claude Talford said. 'But if we don't bring some sanity to this thing, it's never going to correct itself. It could snowball.'"

Yes, it could.

Chapter 10

HOW GOVERNMENT NEEDS TO CHANGE

Religious organizations became the Dirty Harrys of relief, doing the hard jobs in tough situations—but filmdom's Dirty Harry was on the government payroll, and the acceptance of all those dirty jobs soon led to the question of who would pay for the extraordinary expenses incurred. As the *Boston Globe* reported after a month of Katrina aid giving, "Churches along with other private organizations have found their resources stretched to an unprecedented degree." The *Houston Chronicle* editorialized in favor of government payments: "Many Houston churches continue to shelter Louisiana refugees and deserve compensation if they can provide proper documentation of their expenses. . . . The extended length of the emergency has stretched the capabilities of some groups to the breaking point, and federal assistance is necessary."

When FEMA announced one month after Katrina that religious organizations, like secular ones, would be eligible for government reimbursement if they operated at government request emergency shelters, food distribution centers, or medical facilities, a heated debate broke out. Americans United for Separation of Church and State attacked the "crass effort by the Bush administration to take advantage of a tragic situation by placating his conservative constituency," and declared (without giving evidence of problems) that evacuees "should not be subjected to unwanted, high-pressure religious coercion."

Many religious groups, for their part, showed no eagerness to grab on to the horns of government money. Robert Reccord of the Southern Baptist Convention stressed that "volunteer labor is just that: volunteer." He said, "We would never ask the government to pay for it." Flip Benham of Operation Save America said he would not apply for government funds: "The people have been so generous to give that for us to ask for reimbursement would be like gouging for gas." Other organizations also said no, stating that their volunteers were working out of a love of God, that they feared an eventual smothering within the federal embrace, and that donors gave precisely because the groups had no other way of getting money.

On the other hand, churches such as Christus Victor Lutheran in Ocean Springs, Mississippi, welcomed the opportunity. About two hundred evacuees and volunteer workers were sleeping each night in the church during the weeks following Katrina's landfall, and four hundred were eating there. When local officials had asked the church to become a shelter, parish administrator Suzie Harvey had immediately agreed: "This was just something we had to do. Later we realized we had no income coming in." While the electric bill and charges for water and other supplies were soaring, nearly one-fourth of the church's six hundred fifty members were homeless and unable to contribute. The church planned to ask FEMA to compensate it for out-of-pocket costs.

CHURCH AND STATE

The debate could rightly be viewed on several levels. First, religious groups needed clarification of what the federal government would pay for. Some poor churches needed help with out-of-pocket costs for food and supplies, but any payment for time spent would create a terrible precedent. The deeper questions involved attitudes toward government-church relations both within Washington and in the country at large. George W. Bush, in 2004, referred to the "culture inside government which resents and fears religious charities, and has discriminated against them." This resentment is magnified within media and academia—partly due to fear and ideological/theological hatred, and partly due to historical ignorance.

I've shown in previous books that statements such as "American evangelicalism has always kept its distance from governmental power" (*New York Times*) are historically inaccurate. Evangelicals have always been politically involved and willing to use governmental power to abolish slavery and, more recently, to fight restrictions on their ability to build poverty-fighting programs. The First Amendment to the U.S. Constitution came into being to provide freedom *for* religion, not freedom *from* religion: the amendment banned any "establishment of religion," which, to a generation that opposed Britain's establishment, meant giving official preference to a particular religious denomination.

For over a century and a half the consensus summarized by de Tocqueville in the 1830s held firm: "Americans combine the notions of Christianity and of liberty so intimately in their minds that it is impossible to make them conceive the one without the other." But the U.S. Supreme Court, in its 1947 *Everson v. Board of Education* decision, resurrected the idea of a "wall of separation" between church and state—the phrase occurs in an 1802 letter by Thomas Jefferson—from 145 years of near-entombment. The Court decision itself did not establish a wall but merely ruled that government should be neutral in its relations with religious institutions, giving them neither preferences above nonreligious groups nor treating them as adversaries. Religious groups, the Court said, were eligible for "general government services" as long as the criteria for eligibility were also neutral.

Court rulings since then, including *Lemon v. Kurtzman* (1971), have established a methodology for assessing neutrality, but the essential Court position has not changed in nearly six decades—which means there is no constitutional reason why a secular organization can be compensated for its disaster relief expenses and a religious organization cannot. Nevertheless, media judges, more influential than Judge Wapner or Judge Judy, set off fire alarms about any church involvement in relief efforts. A week after Katrina hit, *CBS Early Show* cohost Harry Smith raised questions about the prospects of religious families hosting nonreligious evacuees: "Do I need to be concerned that I'm going to go live with a church family, are they going to proselytize me, are they going to say, 'You better come to church with me or else, I'm, you know, you're not going to get your breakfast this morning'?"

No one provided evidence of that happening, but Americans still seemed to be in a pickle. Our society's ability to react to disaster requires vast involvement by faith-based organizations that can elicit millions of volunteer hours and a willingness to endure hard conditions to help those in need. Direct governmental financing is suspect among both secularists and religious leaders, but churches at the front lines of disaster relief need support. Many media and academic leaders stare at religious groups, especially Christian ones, across the river of suspicion that Harry Smith's questioning represented.

This was not the first time that postdisaster soundings showed such fear of Christian involvement. In the wake of the Columbine school killings in Colorado in 1999, *Wall Street Journal* columnist Peggy Noonan observed, "A gun and a Bible have a few things in common. Both are small, black, have an immediate heft and are dangerous—the first to life, the second to the culture of death." She then quoted a talk-show caller who noted, "Those kids were sick and sad, and if a teacher had talked to one of them and said, 'Listen, there's a way out, there really is love out there that will never stop loving you, there's a real God and I want to be able to talk to you about him'—if that teacher had intervened that way, he would have been hauled into court."

The very next day, the *Wall Street Journal* printed a letter in response: "I profoundly wish Peggy Noonan were right, [but] have we forgotten Jim Jones of Jonestown, who convinced parents that it was God's will to put cyanide into their children's Kool-Aid? Or the killing in the Balkans, where weapons are being blessed by priests?" It's been this way for years: mention something positive done in the name of the God of the Bible, and someone will always mention something negative and attempt to minimize religion's public role. The grudging appreciation for religious Dirty Harrys runs up against the demand that they be kept in their place and not seen as alternatives to governmental incompetence.

The year 1999 also witnessed the beginning of a concentrated attempt to bridge the river of suspicion—George W. Bush's faith-based initiative, which he campaigned for beginning that year and institutionalized once becoming president. Seven years later, the legislative part of that initiative had failed, but the failure points to an alternative that could leave the United States better prepared to deal with the next big disaster.

A DIFFICULT INITIATIVE

Let's trace the lessons, starting with the origin of the initiative in 1999. It was clear then that providing grants to religious groups on the same basis as secular groups would excite hostility from entrenched interests, and would also not be grabbed on to by many of the groups themselves out of concern that they would have to be silent. The Bush campaign task force that looked into the matter concluded that three types of leadership—verbal, organizational, and legislative—would be needed to end governmental discrimination against religious groups that provide social services.

First, an elected George W. Bush would need to speak regularly about the importance of faith in God in poverty fighting and other social concerns. He would need to emphasize the positives of faith-based organizations and argue that faith-based organizations need the freedom to implement their religious programs without imprisonment by the secular definition of social service provision. He would need to point out repeatedly that the aim was not to grant preferences to religious groups, but to stop discrimination against them.

Second, he would need to create, within the executive office of the president, an office that would expose discrimination within current laws and regulations, be a national clearinghouse for information on effective faith-based groups, and serve as an ombudsman for faith-based groups that need help in regard to any federal action. He would need to create similar offices within key federal departments, and also push for states to establish their own faith-based offices. He could use executive orders to change regulations that kept religious groups from being treated on an equal basis with secular nonprofits.

Third, and most important if the faith-based initiative were to be more than a one-administration wonder, President Bush would need to work with Congress to pass new laws to create such equal treatment—but that would be difficult. Given the fast-flowing river of suspicion, bills that allowed religious groups to receive grants for social services would not survive unless they contained restrictions on religious instruction and evangelism within programs, and unless they required conservative churches to hire applicants who did not share the goals of their employers. Any such restrictions, though, would defeat the purpose of the bills by not giving religious organizations equal treatment with secular ones, and by reinforcing the suspicion of many religious groups that working with government requires fatal compromises.

Analysts within the Bush camp differed regarding both principles and tactics. Some thought that religious groups featuring worship, religious teaching, or evangelism as integral parts of their social services program should be ineligible for government grants. Others suggested that government bodies should not pay for lunchtime preaching at a homeless shelter, but could pay for the food and the electricity to cook the food and light the rooms.

Those with a decentralized orientation, though, were unsatisfied with either approach. They argued that the decision of what to allow should not be made by officials but by the people using religion-based social services or paying for them. These advocates proposed giving vouchers to the needy and tax credits to givers. One specific proposal was to create a program of tax credits of up to $250 ($500 for married couples filing joint returns) for cash contributions to poverty-fighting charitable organizations that offered direct services to the poor.

Following five weeks of postelection trauma at the end of 2000, Karl Rove and other high-level Bush officials decided to use the faith-based initiative to cut into the Democratic Party's base and create strategic grants that could attract support from black clergymen, who already disagreed with Democrats on social issues such as abortion and homosexuality. They found an academic who on the basis of principle would support their political goals: John DiIulio, a neoliberal University of Pennsylvania professor with strong ties to the two groups Rove and company chose to appeal to— Northeastern media and East Coast African-American churches.

LEGISLATIVE FAILURE

One immediate legislative result of the Rove plan was that the Bush tax-cut measures introduced in Congress had no mention of any poverty-fighting tax credit or voucher proposals. The Bush economic proposals and the faith-based proposals were on separate and unequal tracks. Rhetorically, though, President Bush got off to a good start early in 2001 by speaking about the importance of faith-based programs and creating an office in the White House to examine discrimination against religious programs and develop equal-access regulations. The big surprise was his choice to head the office: not former Indianapolis mayor Steve Goldsmith, who had helped to develop many of the ideas, but DiIulio.

DiIulio, like the White House politicos, did not like voucher or tax-credit approaches that put the decision making into the hands of ordinary people. Instead, he believed that the right government officials, those firmly based in social science research, could do scientific grant making—no pork, just optimal efficiency. DiIulio's press relations, nonconservative ideology, and obvious sincerity gave the faith-based initiative a generally positive media portrayal at first, and in February 2001 staffers in the faith-based suite of offices next to the White House were padding around on clean carpets with new badges on chains around their necks.

The badge photos captured the deer-in-the-headlight look of driver's license art, which was appropriate since vehicles from many directions soon began trying to run them down. Pundits on the left quickly pressed Uncle Sam-I-am: *Will you fund green eggs and ham? Is all this faith-based stuff a sham? Will some church get a new computer? Will that be OK with David Souter?* Initiative opponents argued that churches were so strong that they would take over government but so weak that government would take over them.

The *New York Times* front-paged a new dimension with a scare story about Scientologists possibly tapping federal funds. Pat Robertson jumped at that bait: "What if cultists want a grant? Should my taxes fund their grant?" Trying to pick up support from the center and left, administration and congressional leaders crafted legislation that required participating religious organizations to sign agreements stating that no federal money would go to any program that included religious teaching. For example, a Jewish or Christian program that stressed the importance of diligent work by quoting Peter Drucker could receive a grant, but citing a verse from the book of Proverbs would make it ineligible.

That stance didn't create enthusiasm for the faith-based initiative among many faith-based poverty fighters. Only 4 percent of evangelical homeless shelter leaders surveyed by *World* in June 2001 favored the administration's grant-making emphasis. Four out of five groups said they would not segment their programs into "religious" and "nonreligious" parts to become eligible for government aid, if that again became a stipulation.

By June 2001 it was also apparent that the Beltway strategy of appeasing liberals by weakening the faith-based bill was not working. The legislation's stipulation that the federal government would not pay for worship, religious teaching, or proselytizing was not enough for those on the left, because under the proposed law, Washington could still pay for food, utilities, or other material costs of a program engaged in those activities. Liberals pushed for more, demanding that to receive funding a religious group would have to be willing to hire gays. That, of course, was anathema to Christian conservatives.

After President Bush went to the Capitol to make a personal appeal to wavering Republicans, the House of Representatives, on virtually a party-line vote, passed what remained of the faith-based bill, without the gay rights amendment—but key senators said they would insist on it. John DiIulio resigned in late August after seven months on the job and later attacked the Bush administration, calling it a haven for "Mayberry Machiavellis."

Then came the events of September 11, 2001, and the attention of the administration and the nation necessarily turned from domestic concerns to the international battle against terrorism. The faith-based initiative stalled legislatively and was still stalled in early 2006, at the time of this writing.

President Bush took what action he could, signing executive orders that temporarily accomplished part of what could have been achieved legislatively. In doing so he stated that "government can and should support social services provided by religious people . . . faith-based programs should not be forced to change their character or compromise their mission." One of his little-noticed statements late in 2002 emphasized the role of religious groups after disasters: he ordered FEMA to "revise its policy on emergency relief so that religious nonprofit groups can qualify for assistance after disasters like hurricanes and earthquakes."

The White House offered up Seattle Hebrew Academy as the type of group that would now be treated like other social service organizations that suffered disaster damage. The academy, along with dozens of other nonprofit organizations, had costs arising from the Nisqually earthquake—a Richter 6.8 that had rocked the Seattle area in 2001—and the Bush administration argued that since disaster relief laws were written so broadly, no First Amendment barrier to helping the Jewish organization existed.

The wording by Jay S. Bybee of the U.S. Department of Justice was important: "There is little exercise of discretion regarding religion in the distribution of grant funds—indeed, in this instance, funding was virtually automatic—and the diverse makeup of those that have received funds confirms that the program's administration is not 'skewed towards religion.' . . . The array of institutions funded by FEMA confirms that the program is neutral in practice. . . . We see no basis for concern that FEMA administrators have discretion to favor religious applicants, or that those administrators have exercised what little discretion they do have in a manner that favors religion."

FROM DISCRETION TO FORMULA

"Automatic," "neutral," "little discretion." These were the words that made funding constitutional, in Bybee's opinion, but they cut against the DiIulio emphasis on discretionary grant making—an emphasis that largely remained in place after his departure and subsequent attack on the Rove operation as a haven for "Mayberry Machiavellis." Late in 2003 the Department of Health and Human Services and the Department of Housing and Urban Development finalized regulations allowing faith-based organizations access to compete for $28 billion in grant money "while maintaining their religious identity." Federal officials would choose the winners, and that raised new concerns among secularists.

At the same time, though, the administration finally began to embrace a social services voucher approach. Those entering antialcoholism and addiction programs could proffer vouchers to pay their way, and soon broadly interpreted voucher approaches began popping up elsewhere. For example, the Department of Labor stated that those who receive job-training vouchers could use them not only at barber schools and truck-driving academies but also at institutions that prepared them for employment with churches or other religious organizations.

President Bush kept asking Congress to act "so people of faith can know that the law will never discriminate against them again." On January 15, 2004, speaking at a New Orleans church, he stated well the problem for religious groups: "Government policy says, on the one hand, perhaps you can help; on the other hand, you can't practice your faith. Faith-based programs are only effective because they do practice faith. It's important for our government to understand that." Nevertheless, Congress refused to move, because the river of suspicion remained high and because fears of governmental preference for one or another religious group remained, as did fears among the religious institutions themselves.

The Seattle Hebrew Academy grant pointed to a way out of this dilemma that could be directly applied to disaster relief funding: emphasize formula grants rather than discretionary ones. Under formula grants, money and resources are provided on the basis of objective, nondiscretionary standards to groups performing defined social services. For example, in nondisaster situations, formula grant programs might provide a computer for every given number of students enrolled in a qualified school, or an ultrasound machine for a given number of pregnant women served. The Supreme Court upheld the constitutionality of such formula grant programs in *Mitchell v. Helms*, so there would be no problem, after disasters, in giving churches like Christus Victor in Mississippi a certain small amount for each person housed, allowing it to recoup its out-of-pocket expenses.

The good news about formula grants is that they function like voucher programs; they don't enhance the discretionary authority of government officials toward religious institutions. They pose little threat to religious liberty, unlike discretionary grant programs that give government officials great power by allowing them to discriminate subtly and unsubtly among grant applicants. Those risks are especially great when programs grow from a few "demonstration projects" into a standardized system, under which hundreds of thousands of grants are awarded by largely unmonitored mid-level government officials.

Much of the hostility toward the faith-based initiative, among both the religious and the secular, has emphasized the prospect of bias. If that fear dissipates, the impasse could end. To avoid the risks of bias, the federal government should not give grants to faith-based groups that pay for overhead costs or the core facilities of an organization. That is the road to dependence on government, with faith-based groups gradually becoming unable to reject the improper demands of funding agencies. Nor should discretionary grants pay for the salaries of persons employed by grant-sponsoring churches or church groups in a teaching or decision-making capacity. That is the road to giving government power over key hiring or firing decisions. Formula grants are neutral.

OTHER OPPORTUNITIES

In the wake of Katrina, voucher approaches also made a comeback. As discussed in chapter 7, criticism of FEMA trailer camps propelled a drive to use rental vouchers that would allow people to move into vacant homes anywhere in the country, giving them the opportunity to make a new start rather than wither in fenced-in camps far from job opportunities. The Bush administration's post-Katrina plan also included vouchers for some students to attend private or religious schools.

Many tax code changes could also boost contributions to disaster responders, but one in particular would be useful to some of the most self-sacrificing helpers, those willing to give an evacuated family refuge in their own homes. Colonial town councils sometimes paid out-of-pocket costs of citizens who housed or fed victims of emergencies. They saw such payments not as compromising the volunteer spirit but as allowing the poor as well as the rich to offer help. The United States could now do the same by providing tax credits (applicable to Social Security as well as income taxes) to all individuals who take evacuees into their homes for extended periods.

That would make it financially possible for the black single mom quoted earlier, and middle-class individuals as well, to help evacuees over long periods of time. It was not logical to have tax deductions for financial contributions but no tax recognition of the far greater commitment that sharing a home represents. Nevertheless, a Congress committed to deficit spending showed little enthusiasm for allowing small decreases of tax payments.

Congress did show some interest in legislation to reduce slightly the power of paperocracy. The GIVE (Good Samaritan Liability Improvement and Volunteer Encouragement) Act of 2005, introduced by Senator John Cornyn (R-TX) would allow medical and other professionals licensed in their home state to provide disaster relief in other states. It would protect other individual volunteers not affiliated with an organization from lawsuits and would also protect donors of goods or equipment, filling gaps left by the Volunteer Protection Act of 1997. Cornyn said he was especially moved by the story of a doctor from Pennsylvania who came to Louisiana to help hurricane victims and was ordered to stop treating patients because he wasn't registered with FEMA, whose officials apparently feared being sued.

It was also important to remove other legal barriers to compassionate activity. For example, in 2004 a plan to have New Orleans churchgoers give rides to residents without cars fell short, in part because of litigation concerns. "Operation Brother's Keeper," after starting up in four congregations, stopped because of concerns that church members who gave their neighbors rides outside the city could face legal liability if something went wrong. In

2004 the state senate passed a law that would release drivers from liability during a hurricane emergency, but Louisiana's House of Representatives did not approve it: some members complained that a drunk driver transporting an evacuee could escape responsibility for an accident. When Katrina struck, the program was dormant.

Some legislators planned to revive such legislation in 2006, and such measures would be both useful and achievable. To deal with larger questions, though, the need—as Senator Rick Santorum (R-PA) acknowledged—is for "politicians like me to have to start saying some hard truths." He said, "There are things that government can't afford to do as much anymore. Everyone running for office likes to promise everything while saying it will cost nothing. But that is Willy Wonka politics. We are going to have to look at everything from pork to entitlements and make some tough decisions about changing the role of government in our lives."

Chapter 11

HOW THE CHURCH NEEDS TO CHANGE

Changes in government can create a level playing field for religious and nonreligious institutions, but religious institutions—and we'll look here particularly at Christian ones, given the makeup of America—will also need to change if they are to face the challenges brought by Katrina or other disasters. Some will have to start referring to "we sinners" rather than "you sinners." Some will need to fight the perception, and sometimes the reality, that they put law before grace and morality before faith. Some will need to think more deeply about how they can be a blessing to the whole community.

Non-Christians now typically believe that Christianity takes away freedom rather than adds to it. I sometimes ask students at the first meeting of my University of Texas course on Journalism and Religion to answer on paper (while I read the roll) this question: "How do Christians act?" When

I request top-of-the-head, anonymous responses, typical answers are: "Fanatical"; "Cram religion down others' throats"; "Want to push their religion on others"; "Trying to force others to do everything their way"; "Bossing, not helping, others."

The cartoon version of conservative Christianity presented in mainstream media contributes to that stereotype, but it partly reflects the actions of fringe fundamentalists who have given liberal journalists plenty of ammunition. Like the rest of us, journalists have seen video clips of a small group that appears at gay gathering places to yell, "God hates fags." Those pictures stick in the heads of many liberals, particularly those unaware of the work of evangelicals who help homosexuals stricken with AIDS.

Football coaches say, "You play as you practice," and that's also true for response to disaster: what people do in normal times shows what they'll do amid crisis. For example, chapter 6 noted a post-Katrina attack on New Orleans by Michael Marcavage, leader of a little group called Repent America. Finger pointing after disaster is exactly what would be expected from a Christian who regularly shows up at gay festivals and denounces homosexuals through bullhorns. Marcavage considers it a badge of honor when lesbians call him a "fascist" and the *Philadelphia Inquirer* quotes his message as, "We're just here to warn youand judgment dayand atonementand sin."

The spacing in the sentence above was the *Inquirer*'s way of indicating that meaning was lost in the tirade; the newspaper was obviously biased but probably representing the attitudes of most Philadelphia readers. A Barna poll in 2004 showed that only 44 percent of non-Christians had a positive view of Christian ministers, and only 22 percent had a positive view of evangelicals generally. A better way to discuss a clear biblical wrong such as homosexuality comes from Herb Lusk, pastor of Greater Exodus Baptist Church. Lusk, an ex-NFL tailback who preached regularly to the prostitutes who used to close deals on his doorstep, says biblical opposition to homosexuality "should be preached without apology, [but] has to be coupled with love and compassion or there's a problem with it."

CHANGING THE PICTURE

Evangelical problems go deeper than a few screamers at the edge. Major churches have at times promulgated rules against dancing, card playing, listening to particular types of music, drinking a beer, and so on, and treated these rules as God-given rather than man-made. Such restrictions have a long heritage; Oliver Cromwell created a backlash by imposing some in England during the 1650s. They may emerge from good motives and for reasons similar to those developed by Orthodox Jews: set up the fence so far away from the border that there is no possibility of stepping over. And yet they produce confusion about what is of God and what is of man.

These restrictions are now rare, but many journalists who don't set foot in churches still think that just about every church has them. These tendencies and others lead to press stereotypes of Christians, some of which are accurate. Mockery (including self-mockery) is the leading form of humor for David Letterman and others on the airwaves after early-to-rise folks have gone to bed, and Christians do tend to be straight-laced by contemporary standards. That's all for the good, as long as the laces keep our shoes on and don't trip us up. But often they do, and Christians need to go by the Bible and not nineteenth-century custom.

The stylistic difference between many evangelicals and the many journalists trained on David Letterman–mockery also has an impact. Many media secularists look down on Christians so aching with a sincere desire to reach non-Christians that they start talking *at* them rather than reasoning *with* them. Many journalists tell privately of their experience with evangelicals who, not taking no for an answer, pushed even harder when rejection was apparent. So some of the tension is inevitable—and yet contrast the impression left (in different ways) by the Marcavages and the Lettermans with the impression left by thousands of Christians in the wake of Katrina.

For example, the *New York Times* described how at the Allen Chapel A.M.E. Church in Baton Rouge, forty evacuees slept in the church's sanctuary, ten in the ushers' room, eight in the library, and a dozen in the choir area. The pastor said "All we wanted to do was try to help in any way we can. We're doing it from the fact that God wants us to do this." That motivation was more powerful than a paycheck in leading church people to put in round-the-clock hours, and the testimony of action led many people to ask, "Why are you volunteering?" When pastors and volunteers answered in that context, even the *Times* temporarily put aside its objections to evangelizing: "After members of Southern Baptist disaster response teams from North Carolina finish clearing debris or doing temporary repairs on damaged houses in Gulfport, Mississippi, they give the homeowners a signed Bible and say a prayer with them."

This is the best evangelism in modern America. Ancient Israel was a holiness theme park, with laws laid down by Moses fencing off a holy people separated from others and dedicated to God. The land itself was a theme park, with everything (geography, economics, laws, customs) stressing holiness—although in the end, all those aids to reverence proved insufficient. America, though, is a liberty theme park, and Christians here evangelize most successfully when people come to understand that the prime Christian objective is to add to their lives, not subtract.

Many of my students understand at some level that liberty without virtue becomes license, and licentiousness leads to anarchy. Many are the children of sexual liberty that has led to divorce or single parenting, so they don't have familial constancy in their lives. The upbringing of most has been postmodern, with no clear sense of right and wrong. Most want liberty and desperately want it now, but at the same time they understand at some level that liberty by itself is not the answer: if a generation ago Joan Baez sang that the answer was blowin' in the wind, many Americans have learned that liberty gained in a gust is only the liberty of leaves.

A low-key approach is needed for such wanderers. A low-key approach is also thoroughly biblical in settings where those who believe in God are outside the Holy Land and in a minority. The Jeremiah who assaulted ears within the borders of ancient Judah told the exiles in Babylon that they were to settle down, build houses, and plant gardens. Instead of calling down curses on Babylon, they were to remember that they were part of it and should pray for it, for "in its welfare you will find your welfare."

God did not tell His people to spend much of their time in counterdemonstrations in front of idol-laden temples. He also did not tell them to lose their distinctiveness and melt into the surrounding community: Daniel offered advice to Babylonian rulers, and in the book of Esther, Mordecai found how to use Persian law and custom to preserve his people. The New Testament exhibits the same pattern of standing firm on rights and proclaiming the gospel at every opportunity but not calling for insurrection or giving up. The apostle Paul demanded not revolution but his rights as a Roman citizen. He told Corinthian believers, living in one of the empire's most dissolute cities, "Be strong. Let all that you do be done in love" (1 Cor. 16:13-14).

We rarely see strength and love put together in this way, but Paul did so appropriately because he was teaching people to walk in the steps of Christ, who was harsh to ostentatiously religious Pharisees but gentle with those outside of Israel, like the Samaritan woman (John 4) and the Syro-Phoenician woman (Mark 7). Except to Pharisee leaders who invented laws beyond those biblically demanded, Jesus was calm rather than clamorous, beckoning rather than beheading.

WHO IS MY NEIGHBOR?

Jesus also expanded understandings of responsibilities to others as He told of the Good Samaritan and asked the question, "Who is my neighbor?" The Jewish answer to that question was at the most "your fellow Jew," and more often just the Jews who lived close by. Jesus, though, ate with tax collectors and others seen as "sinners" and taught that anyone in need is our neighbor. He added women, Samaritans, and even enemy soldiers to the list of God's people.

The first three words of the Constitution form a secularized version of Christ's expansiveness: "We, the people." Christianity has been the outstanding vehicle in human history for increasing the liberty of people lacking in power: women, the poor, the sick, the aged, the enslaved in the nineteenth century, racial minorities in the twentieth century, and now the not-yet-born. Certainly, some Christians defended slavery and discrimination, but they were doing what was common in much of the world: the sensational news is that a critical mass of Christians has fought for what was uncommon.

Each century since the ratification of the Constitution has raised questions of "Who is my neighbor?" or "Who is included in 'We, the People'?" The big nineteenth-century experiment was whether neighbors from different religions could gain acceptance. As millions of Catholic and Jewish immigrants arrived from Ireland, Italy, and eastern Europe, some ugly nativist groups sprung up and some Christians sadly joined them, for those who thought of their country as a holy land fought what they saw as pollution by millions of immigrants. Nevertheless, by the end of the century the consensus was clear: the neighborhood could include Catholics and Jews, and soon a smattering of Buddhists, Hindus, and Muslims as well.

The big twentieth-century experiment was whether members of different racial and ethnic groups should be considered neighbors. The Civil War hadn't settled that, since African-Americans largely moved from slavery to sharecropping, which did not leave many any better off. In the mid-twentieth century, many strong and courageous Christians fought for civil rights as many of their predecessors had fought for emancipation. In India Hindu priests lead the opposition against equal rights for the dark-skinned Dalits ("untouchables"), but in the United States ministers like Martin Luther King and others of the Southern Christian Leadership Conference argued that both whites and blacks should sit down at the table of brotherhood.

As we have seen, some journalists attributed much of the damage in New Orleans to racism or at least a lack of neighborly caring. A *New York Times* editorial on September 1, the worst day at the Convention Center, asked, "Why was Congress, before it wandered off to vacation, engaged in slashing the budget for correcting some of the gaping holes in the area's flood protection?" One month later *Times* critic Nicholas Ouroussoff argued that the failure to shore up levees was "an outgrowth of the campaign against 'big government' that helped propel Ronald Reagan to the presidency 25 years ago." He continued, "And it was fueled by uglier motives, including a latent fear of cities, a myth of the city as a breeding ground for immorality."

Those who followed the money trail, though, came to different conclusions. John Fund of the *Wall Street Journal* explained in January 2006 how "earmarks" (pork projects crammed into spending bills) hurt New Orleans: "In Louisiana, the Army Corps of Engineers spent $1.9 billion between 2000 and 2005, more than 80% of which was earmarked. Less than 4% of the total was spent on protecting levees, while over a third of the money went to building a new lock on an underused canal." At that rate it would have taken $25 billion of new appropriations to get $1 billion spent on levees.

If we think of others as neighbors, we don't leave them unprotected in order to pay off political contributors or allies with earmarked dollars.

Eliminating earmarks would help, but even if such a reform bill would be passed, it would not be long before something of that kind returned. As long as sweet rolls are on the table in the summertime, flies will buzz around them. We can accomplish some things, but we can't expect government (based on power and attracted by money) to start suddenly acting out of love. Successful reaction to disaster is more likely if churches become centers for treating as neighbors those who have been displaced.

PREPARING FOR DISASTER

How to start? As Southern Baptist relief specialists have shown, churches can let local government and the local American Red Cross know of their willingness to shelter a certain number of people should a nearby disaster arise. They can offer the use of church kitchens or provide space for mobile feeding or meal distribution sites.

A church can also offer to be a distribution center for clothing or bulk food items, an information staging area for volunteers or work units, a child-care facility, or an information and communication center. Church members can be ready to provide transportation, assist with cleanup and repair, and provide counseling. A church can prepare for disastrous times by setting up everyday poverty-fighting ministries (as the next chapter will show) and by helping out in small-scale but deep local crises: fires, accidents, crimes.

A church can have in place a disaster relief committee with a leader in charge and prepared to give direction. The committee can survey church members' skills, gifts, talents, and willingness to serve; provide regular, up-to-date training; plan for making facilities and equipment available when disaster strikes; begin and maintain a crisis closet and food pantry; build links with other churches and civic groups, local government officials, and the American Red Cross; and develop a database of cars, vans, pickup and dump trucks, and boats that might be available for use during a disaster.

Churches can be prepared when there is a disaster to provide or purchase cleanup or repair products and make grants or loans for emergency needs. Members can offer legal or business advice regarding insurance, repair contracts, and applications for loans or grants. Members can care for children, the elderly, the ill, or the disabled; provide temporary housing and community orientation for those who have been displaced; assist with those who have language or literacy limitations; and collect, sort, and distribute clothing, bedding, bulk food, and household supplies. Churches can provide food, housing, and other help for out-of-town volunteers, and organize cleanup, salvage, security, or repair crews.

As churches organize, there's a lot to think through and pray about. Churches need to consider the risks their community is most likely to face and to recognize that it is more likely that a disaster will occur far away— in which case a church facility can be a gathering point for food, supplies, building materials, and other items; an orientation center for untrained people who have volunteered to help in the disaster area; or a staging area for mobile units en route to the disaster site. Many churches will want to link with others in their denomination or area.

Churches also need to consider finances: both how to maintain a low level of disaster ministry during normal times and how to pay for what could be urgent escalation with very short notice. Many Christians do what they feel called to do regardless of the economic costs, but those realities can increase or decrease effectiveness. Some churches in hurricane areas, for example, could have chain saws and tree removal equipment; those located near homes for the elderly might have some wheelchairs and walkers available. What's key is a desire to serve, and that often begins with preaching and teaching, as the next chapter suggests.

Chapter 12

ONE CHURCH'S EXPERIENCE

Three weeks after Katrina hit, ABC *Good Morning America* reporter Ron Claiborne voiced over a clip: "Janice Sturm, a white woman from Leesburg, Florida, and Jonique Bazile, an African-American woman, now formerly from New Orleans. It is an unlikely friendship formed from a disaster." The clip showed Janice Sturm saying about Bazile and herself, "We're bonded for life," with Janice's husband, Norm Sturm, adding the new relationship was "just like family." Bazile concluded, "They love hugs and they love the children."

Claiborne gave the back story: "When Hurricane Katrina struck New Orleans, Jonique, her husband, Michael, and their two children had to flee their home. Like so many other evacuees, they ended up in a shelter in Mississippi, cut off from family and friends, with no money, no prospects." Then a pastor told them about "Leesburg, a place they'd never even heard of. When they landed, they were greeted like family by strangers, members of the First Baptist Church of Leesburg, which had helped to arrange for their move."

Claiborne voiced over more film: "Janice Sturm and her husband, Norm, volunteered to be the Baziles' host family, to show them around, help them get settled. For the Bazile family, it's been an astonishing change of fortune. They now have a large furnished apartment. Their girls are in daycare and kindergarten. And with the church's assistance, Michael Bazile got a job at a local lumber company." When Claiborne asked whether they were "surprised that it is white people doing this," Mrs. Bazile answered, "Honestly, yes. Yeah," and Mr. Bazile added, "We've actually gained way more than we ever could have lost."

The Baziles with their two small daughters were one of ten Katrina families that First Baptist decided to host. Tyronne Roussell and Trina Cooper had lived on the west bank of the Mississippi until Hurricane Katrina dumped two feet of water into their home. They and their extended family—Trina's two sisters and parents—came to Leesburg because First Baptist had arranged a home for them to live in for the next year. David and Tanya Sayles, who had worked as a medical technician and an administrative assistant, respectively, came with their eleven-year-old daughter.

AN ORDINARY-LOOKING CHURCH

Those families and others also started attending First Baptist, which from the outside looks ordinary. Located about an hour's drive northwest of Orlando on a main street that also boasts a McDonald's, Subway, and Ace Hardware, First Baptist's sanctuary sports a standard denominational look: columned portico, rising steeple, and lots of people, with an average attendance of two thousand two hundred during the winter and one thousand four hundred during the summer. But this ordinary church has been doing some extraordinary things that make the whole community rejoice—and in the process has gained the experience and confidence that helps it respond quickly to disasters.

The church's efforts begin with senior pastor Charles Roesel, a sixty-eight-year-old who runs three miles a day. One Sunday morning in 2005 he bounded up the steps to the pulpit and spoke of how the sixth commandment, which bans murder, also bans "doing nothing when you can save or transform a life." He said, "For too long we've evaluated a church by how many people stream in the front door on a Sunday," and he proposed an alternative: "Evaluate a church by how many people serve the Lord Jesus by serving the hurting all week long."

Roesel argued that God brought disaster on Sodom because its residents were "arrogant, overfed, unconcerned," and then said many of today's churches have also become a "knife and fork club." He said, "We don't spend time with those who are lost, we spend time with each other." He began emphasizing what he calls "ministry evangelism" shortly after becoming the church's pastor in 1976. The church's typical attendance of two hundred leaped to six hundred six months later, but not everyone was on board with the plan to make First Baptist known for its compassion. When the pastor pushed for the church to create a children's home, only 51 percent of congregation members voted for it.

"I backed off and started expository preaching through the New Testament," Roesel recalls. "The centrality of ministry to the needy comes up over and over. I hit it hard." One couple decided to give $25,000 for the children's home, and additional money came in once the home opened in a ramshackle house and stories about the needy children circulated through the congregation. One nine-year-old who came to the home trembled when anyone tried to hug him, didn't know what a bathroom was, and at first slept in the closet rather than on a bed because that was all he knew.

In the 1980s the church also established a crisis pregnancy center and shelters for homeless or troubled men and women in existing buildings, one so ramshackle that (as a church joke went) "if the termites hadn't held hands, it wouldn't have stood up." Compassion was still an add-on at a church headed in the right direction, yet one not yet making major sacrifices for the poor and needy.

By the early 1990s Roesel's preparation of his congregation was complete. Some members spoke of building a larger sanctuary so the church would not need two (now three) worship services on Sunday morning, but when their pastor said he wanted the church instead to build a ministry village with first-class buildings for those in need, members voted unanimously to embrace that vision and without any formal campaign donated $2 million.

"This has been one of the most thrilling adventures of my lifetime," Roesel said. "God did this." What God did at First Baptist is striking not only in the broad range of ministries the church runs, but also in their location smack beside the steepled church. Some churches want their ministries of compassion to be geographically separate from and financially unequal to their worship functions, but First Baptist supports Christ's teaching that loving our neighbor belongs in the same sentence as loving God (Luke 10:27).

PRACTICING MINISTRY EVANGELISM

Just a few hops, skips, and jumps from the front door of the sanctuary are the seven buildings that the church constructed. The facilities, totaling thirty-three thousand six hundred square feet under roof on four acres of land, with a current valuation of over $4 million, include:

- a women's care center decorated in feminine shades of beige and green. It has eighteen beds for women "who are tired of being who they are," according to director Charlotte Tubush. Residents must attend daily Bible study and church on Wednesday and Sunday. Some sing in the choir or participate in the church's nursing home ministry; that furthers the goal of bringing the women into the church community.

- a men's residence decorated in utilitarian cinderblock and linoleum. It has thirty beds for those determined to overcome past addictions. Residents spend four months studying the Bible and taking classes in subjects such as "How to be a man," "How to be financially responsible," and "How to manage anger." They typically spend four months more in getting and holding on to a job, saving money, getting a car, and preparing to move out on their own.

- a pregnancy care center with thirty-five active and regular volunteers who provide free pregnancy testing, medical referrals, nutrition classes, and adoption assistance. Clients who receive ongoing counseling and support pick out their own maternity clothes and receive other assistance.

- a community medical care center that has provided free care to six thousand of the eight thousand low-income, noninsured residents in the church's region. As director Howard Vesser says, "It's on our property, we present Christ to everyone who comes, and Leesburg Regional Hospital gives us a quarter of a million dollars each year because it saves them a fortune: everyone we see is someone they don't have to."

- a residential group home that provides long-term shelter for nine children who have emotional problems that make them unready for foster care and are old enough to make adoption unlikely. Houseparents Mike and Kim McElroy report small but significant victories: after a year, a little boy who wouldn't talk, hug, or hold hands grabbed Mrs. McElroy's hand. An older boy started destroying everything he could, until police came and took him away in handcuffs. Mr. McElroy recalls, "We could have said, 'Don't come back,' but we took him back, and since then he's been a changed person."

- a children's shelter that provides emergency housing for sixteen kids ages six through seventeen. Director Myra Wood, formerly an investigator with the Florida Department of Children and Families, notes that some of the children had "slept in a corner with animal feces," but the shelter offers them quilts on their beds and orderly lives.

- a benevolence center where seventy volunteers help one thousand people a month who come with proof of imminent housing eviction or utility cutoffs, or who fill out information sheets and then receive food and clothing. First Baptist has established limits: financial help once in a six-month period, with payment by voucher rather than cash; a two-day supply of food; eight items of clothing per person.

Those ministries have buildings of their own, but seventy others take place in general purpose church buildings or out in the community. Among them are adoption counseling for birthparents, backyard Bible clubs, Caring Hands deaf ministry, divorce recovery support group, Furniture Barn, Grief Share, Haitian ministry, jail ministry, literacy classes, mother's day out program, nursing home ministry, post-abortion support group, and so on.

First Baptist also houses its own Christian school, First Academy, which has four hundred students and charges tuition of $4,600 per year. The church particularly emphasizes its mentoring program (which includes before- and after-school tutoring), summer reading program, abstinence education, and "Saturday Sunday School," which unites Saturday morning activities and Christ-centered mentoring for poor children.

Not everyone likes the Leesburg approach. Some favor Christian social programs but ask why they should be under church auspices: why not set up specialized social ministries, some of which might use church facilities? That makes sense in some situations; organizations can do things different ways. But some conservative evangelicals oppose any social ministries: given the theological splits that emerged a century ago, they fear creeping social gospelism and worry that concern with poverty or abortion will inhibit evangelism and church growth. Some other critics want sanctuaries to be cathedrals and fear approaches that can get in the way of building plans.

First Baptist opposes those worries with its own strong, biblical preaching and its experience. Before the new emphasis, the church added about thirty members a year through baptism, with new members typically being the children or relatives of those already in the church. Now (to use one measurement of growth) the church regularly baptizes two hundred to three hundred persons each year. Other churches have found involvement with the needy to be both biblically mandated and a contributor to church growth, as some who formerly disparaged church teaching as "pie in the sky" have come to understand its life-changing practicality.

Some other critics of the Leesburg approach prefer broad giveaway programs to the more intensive work the church now emphasizes. To that complaint Don Michael, a retired military pilot who chairs the board of directors that oversees the church's major mercy activities, responds, "Been there, done that." He says, fifteen years ago "we felt like we were enabling people who didn't want to change."

CHURCH-STATE ISSUES

Overall, the church and ministries budget has increased from $180,000 annually in 1979 to $5.5 million in 2005. Forty percent of the expenditures are for the church and the seventy ministries housed within it; 28 percent are for the seven ministries that are housed in their separate buildings on the church grounds; and 32 percent are for the school, which began in 1989.

Those numbers don't include payments and donations by Florida governmental and corporate entities. The residential group home receives from the state $66 per child per night. The medical care center receives substantial funding from Leesburg Regional Hospital, which appoints three members of the center's board; First Baptist appoints four. Disney World donates food, and local supermarkets day-old bread. Pharmaceutical companies annually contribute supplies worth $60,000 to $90,000.

First Baptist members state that such ties do not duct tape the church's voice, and visible evidence shows that. Signs asking, "Where will you spend eternity?" and stating, "Jesus Christ is Lord," are prominent in the clinic's waiting room. Dr. Vesser states, "We ask patients if they'd like to have someone from the church visit them." He notes that the asking is polite: "We make sure they understand it's not a swap."

So far the ACLU and similar groups have not brought suit, and maybe they won't, because ministries such as the community medical care center provide a lot of bang for few bucks. For example, that center's records show that thirty-eight licensed medical professionals each month donate more than three hundred fifty hours with a total monthly value of $50,000; donations of pharmaceuticals, X-rays, lab work, eyeglasses, and so forth, plus the time of forty-two nonlicensed volunteers, totals another $50,000 per month. Overall, with $30,000 for operating expenses cast on the water each month, more than four times as much comes back.

Pastor Roesel emphasizes hands-on ministry, and the more hands the better: "If church leaders feel that they must control everything in the church's ministry, they are unlikely to permit members to use their gifts. . . . Pastors are 'player coaches' [who] affirm, train, and enable members to use their gifts in ministry."

One member who uses her gifts and also her experiences is Wanda Kohn, who in 1977, at age seventeen, had an abortion that she said led to "a hardening," which in turn led her to become "emotionally unattached." Nevertheless, during the 1980s she became a Christian and came to understand that women who had aborted could still receive God's forgiveness. She now directs the church's pregnancy care center and was profiled in 2003 by *Orlando Sentinel* columnist Lauren Ritchie under a headline, "Wanda Kohn—She Is What I Want to Be." She called Kohn "Leesburg's version of Mother Teresa" and began her article by stating, "Once a year, I have lunch with Wanda Kohn to remind myself of what I should be like, if ever I could."

Hands-on ministry is making the church a blessing for the entire community, a church known for adding rather than subtracting. Ritchie wrote that First Baptist of Leesburg "has a tremendous ministry with the most down-on-their-luck people in the county." Since the church does it all the time, it was ready to do it with Katrina evacuees.

First Baptist of Leesburg is an ordinary-looking church with members who, assessed statistically, are not extraordinary. If they can accomplish extraordinary things, so can others.

Part Five

DISASTERS ABROAD

The disaster that has repeatedly resulted in millions of deaths in poor countries, famine, has been unknown in the United States. Four of the seven most death-producing disasters in world history were famine-related: two in China (1333–1347 and 1876–1878), one in India (1896–1901), and one with two phases in the Ukraine (1921–1923 and 1932–1933). At least thirty-four million, and perhaps ten or twenty million more, died in those disasters.

The major Central American disaster of 2005, Hurricane Stan, brought with it rain and flooding that buried some villages under mud and washed others away, with hundreds of thousands left homeless in rural Mayan villages. Nearly three hundred thousand villagers in Guatemala faced hunger after Hurricane Stan's torrents flooded away corn, beans, and topsoil. The villagers would have relished aid that arrived within five days' time, since months later many still were without help. The Associated Press, on December 5, 2005, reported a visit to one Guatemalan village by U.S.

undersecretary of state Karen Hughes, who pledged help. One villager, Gloria Fuentes, told reporters that aid would be nice but "what would help me more would be a visa to go up there," to the United States.

Overall, the historical record shows that, in dealing with disasters, affluence is the best medicine. Cultural superstitions and practices that hold back economic advance contribute to calamity. In previous sections we've concentrated on domestic disasters; now let's look at what has happened in international disasters of not only the kind the United States has but also those we do not have, such as malaria or AIDS within a context of dire poverty. We'll also examine what happens not when government makes a problem worse—which has often been the case recently in Africa and Latin America—but when government *is* the problem.

Chapter 13

FROM TSUNAMIS TO MALARIA

When a Richter scale 9.0 earthquake in the Indian Ocean, in December 2004, led to a wall of water that over seven hours swept the ocean from Africa to Indonesia, one quarter of a million people died. Banda Aceh—an eight-hundred-year-old city at the northwest end of Sumatra and one of the oldest Islamic strongholds in southeastern Asia—suffered the most, with ninety thousand dying there. The BBC reported several days after the disaster and described "masses of rubble and dozens of corpses": "Their bodies are bloated and black, their faces unrecognizable. [One woman] was going from one to the next trying to find her children, absolutely distraught, asking us if we had any more information."

As the news of horror flowed out, financial pledges flowed in: $500 million from Japan's government, $900 million from the U.S. government, over $1 billion more from other governments, plus over $1 billion more in private aid. Press accounts of the results, though, showed dismal results.

For example, the *New York Times*, in April 2005, reported: "There is little sign in Aceh of the billions of dollars in donations from governments, aid organizations, civic groups, and individual people who reached out to help from around the world. 'The only thing we've gotten is small packets of food and supplies,' said Samsur Bahri, 54, a shopkeeper who lost his home and now lives with nine people in a small room. 'Where the money is, we don't know. It's just meetings, meetings, meetings.'"

The *Times* reported: "Indonesia's state auditing agency said it was having difficulty accounting for portions of more than $4 billion it says has been received so far in donations, mostly from abroad, as it was being put in the hand of various government agencies. . . . There are no bulldozers or heavy equipment to be seen here; no one is clearing away rubble or repairing roads or bridges; wells are not being decontaminated; power lines are not being put up; there are no sounds of hammers or saws. . . . As the months have passed, the government has been taking a long run-up before it jumps into action. On March 26, well past the original deadline, it issued a draft of what it calls its blueprint for rehabilitation and reconstruction . . . it comes in 12 volumes. Even lawyers and aid officials say it is a challenge to read. For the people here who simply want to start rebuilding their homes, it is baffling."

Four months later, relief efforts were still being held back by, as the *National Catholic Reporter* noted, "policies of the Indonesian government that are often as chaotic as they are contradictory, and brazen attempts by local authorities to extort more money." The central government kept producing plans, then readjusting them, and then postponing issuance of new plans. The government stipulated a minimum size and minimum cost of each new house yet did not rebuild a single one, as projects needed reams of official papers, all appropriately stamped. Meanwhile the Indonesia parliament debated (in July) how more than $125 million of housing aid had mysteriously "disappeared." Banda Aceh governor Mawardy Nurdin, quoted in August, was irate: "For the refugees alone we need 20,000 houses. Until today 20 have been built. The central government doesn't pay anything, the bureaucracy paralyzes us."

As in the United States, one result of misspent relief funds was an increase in cynicism and "compassion fatigue." Americans personally contributed hundreds of millions of dollars to the relief effort, yet a CNN poll showed that 80 percent of all Americans said that they had profound doubts that the money would ever reach those who needed it. One year after the tsunami, many people were still desperate, but the *New York Times* reported that big "aid agencies are present in full force." The article continued, "Overpriced hotels are regularly overbooked. The best homes have been converted into headquarters and guest houses."

Deceit appeared not only in high places but in low ones as well. A *Los Angeles Times* story reported "enough food and supplies [are] coming in to meet the basic needs of tsunami victims here, yet many still go wanting." Many poor Banda Aceh residents, like their counterparts in Jackson, Mississippi, took not what they needed but what they could get. Although in Indonesia the issues were not consumer electronics but more big bags of rice, and not false descriptions of damage to homes but listing for aid those who already had died or moved away.

MILITARY AND RELIGIOUS HELP

As in the United States following Katrina, military performance was better than the performance of civilian officials. Indonesian soldiers showed up quickly at Banda Aceh and other hard-hit areas, but the heroics of American helicopter pilots from the aircraft carrier *Abraham Lincoln* impressed even the BBC. The pilots delivered tons of food, water, medicines, and tents to tsunami victims and showed their disdain for paperocracy by disregarding an Indonesian government command to stop rescuing injured villagers once the Banda Aceh hospital was full. Instead, pilots brought dozens of the injured to a field station quickly set up by navy doctors.

The U.S. military flew at least twenty-eight hundred relief missions around Banda Aceh, often through heavy rain, and treated twenty-two hundred patients. Navy helicopter crews used every bit of daylight and set records for flight hours. They maximized carrying capacity by removing seats and other equipment. They also helped out in devastated Sri Lanka, where the USS *Duluth* and other American ships arrived with earthmoving equipment, two dozen helicopters, and bottled water.

Governments of other tsunami-hit countries also deployed their own soldiers. India refused outside help and relied on thousands of its troops and dozens of its aircraft and ships to evacuate about six hundred fifty thousand people and drop food packets in affected areas. Relief and recovery lagged in India, Sri Lanka, and Thailand, though, as paperocracy ruled. The *National Catholic Reporter* reported about "newly constructed houses sitting empty for weeks because beneficiaries had not been selected, about donations of fishing boats sitting idle because fisherman lacked nets and gear, about aid agencies sitting idle because they lack government authorization to proceed."

Government officials repeatedly hampered the efforts of Christian relief organizations, even ones that did no "proselytizing." In Sri Lanka Caritas was able to begin construction on six thousand transitional shelters but could not proceed with an additional twenty thousand because the government would not allocate land for construction. And yet one Sri Lankan story in the *Washington Post* made explicit the importance of spiritual needs. A husband and wife whose three children drowned in the tsunami fell into unshakable depression, and the husband committed suicide. The wife, Meena Yogeswaran, thirty-one years old, tried to kill herself also but failed. The *Post* said, "She has achieved a kind of peace. She attributes part of her recovery to the teachings of Christianity, to which she converted not long after the disaster."

In Muslim Indonesia, though, imams and Muslim judges followed the traditional Islamic pattern of blaming all or some of the victims for what had happened to them. For example, Indonesian judge Marluddin Jalil said the tsunami came "because of the sins of the people" and particularly those of women: "The Holy Koran says that if women are good, then a country is good." Some evangelical organizations tried to provide a different interpretation, but they were unwelcome by officials. Radical Muslims killed several Christians, in one case leaving a severed head in front of a church.

This was tragic for many reasons: one is that, apart from spiritual and psychological change, it seems that material aid helps only a little and may at times make things worse. One year after the tsunami the *Washington Post* reported that in the Sri Lankan fishing village of Navalady "more than half its remaining fishermen have not returned to work, living instead off odd jobs and government handouts, as boats and nets donated by private groups sit idle." One charitable group gave two fishermen "nets and a 21-foot fiberglass outrigger to replace the gear they lost in the tsunami . . . But they have yet to launch the red-and-black boat," and merely sit and drink.

Some international giving was comedic, as "well-intentioned donors," according to the *Los Angeles Times*, "modeled everything on their own country, without necessarily taking into account local social structures." For example, a village "built by Austrian donors, resembles a town in the Alps. . . . Homes bear plaques such as Stiegl Brewery of Salzburg and Austrian Labor Union" But the *Sunday Leader*, a Sri Lankan newspaper, exposed the darker side, reporting, "huge bungling and misallocation of funds" in bank accounts linked to President Mahinda Rajapakse, whose home district was to have 2,253 new houses, although only 1,158 lost their homes there. Opportunism was rampant, with private aid directors reporting, "People not even affected by the tsunami are receiving aid just because they know someone."

In small villages, fishermen like Wijesuriya Patabendige complained that government agents "only give boats and nets to family members, friends or those who pay bribes. There's a complaint office, but it's staffed by the same people asking for bribes. We want our livelihoods back." Others worried about another unintended consequence from the well-intentioned torrent of aid. Consultant Palitha Abeykoon said, "I think we're creating a begging culture. Everything is free, people come for breakfast, lunch, take a nap, all at the camps, then get a $5 handout. It's no good, like giving a hungry man a bottle of whisky."

Material damage and especially the human toll after the tsunami were much greater than that following Katrina, so it's no surprise that both parents and children throughout 2005 were depressed and suffering from post-traumatic stress syndrome. That's especially so because poverty reigns and business opportunity is often lacking. (Wal-Martization would be a great improvement in many places, but it's years off.) Furthermore, disease often follows disaster: those who survived the tsunami had to fight another wave, this one of diseases such as malaria, dengue, and others spread by insects.

FIGHTING MALARIA

In this respect, World Health Organization (WHO) officials in Southeast Asia also became part of the problem. Many people would have benefited from having the walls of their homes sprayed with tiny amounts of DDT so as to create a chemical barrier that mosquitoes wouldn't cross. They couldn't get that done because the anti-DDT campaign of the 1960s—which led to abandonment of the insecticide in Western countries and then in most of the rest of the world—is still a cornerstone of WHO's way of doing business.

The history here is sad. Because of DDT spraying, malaria in Sri Lanka fell from three million cases a year in the 1940s to fewer than fifty in 1963. Since the abandonment of DDT, the incidence of malaria has increased again, especially when inadequate nutrition and physical degradation present particularly receptive targets. Research over the past four decades has knocked down much of the case against DDT since the 1960s, and what remains is a warning against the agricultural use of massive amounts of DDT. But WHO has been obdurate to this point.

DDT bans have also hurt the worldwide fight against malaria, which affects five hundred million people each year and kills one million. Nine-tenths of the deaths come in Africa, where malaria is the leading slayer of children under five, killing one every thirty seconds and leaving many survivors brain-damaged. Years ago analysts searched for a reason why malaria hit Africa so much harder than it did other continents, and the reason turned out to be dual: climate plus entomology.

Malaria devastates Africa in part because the continent is so hot, and that's important because the process of transmitting malaria begins when a mosquito bites someone already infected and ingests the malarial parasite. Over a two-week period—or shorter when it's hot—the parasite goes through a transformation called sporogony; once it occurs, the mosquito can infect others. The curious part is that the life span of the mosquito is also two weeks, so in cool areas mosquitoes typically die just before they become infectious. However, in Africa they bite first, die later.

The entomology explains why Africa is hit harder by malaria than, say, Sri Lanka or India. It takes two bites of humans in a row—one for the mosquito to ingest the parasite, the other two weeks later to infect another person—for malaria to be transmitted. In India the predominant mosquito type prefers to bite cattle, but in Africa mosquitoes almost always bite humans. The result is that malaria can be transmitted in Africa nine times more readily than in India.

The devastating result partly explains why Africa lags behind other continents in development: it takes hard effort to come out of poverty, yet malaria creates physical weakness and contributes to fatalistic lassitude. Its effects are so devastating that it would seem any available weapon should be used against malarial mosquitoes—yet DDT, the weapon that eradicated malaria in Europe and the United States more than half a century ago and virtually did the same in Sri Lanka, sits on the shelf.

It didn't always. In the 1950s, as a worldwide antimosquito campaign greatly reduced infestations in Asia and Latin America, three African countries began using it to great effect. But in 1962, before DDT could sweep through Africa and sweep away mosquitoes, biologist Rachel Carson's highly influential book, *Silent Spring* (Houghton Mifflin, 1962), attacked pesticides for causing environmental damage and singled out DDT as the worst offender.

Carson said the chemical was behind the thinning eggshells of some birds and was contributing to fewer hatchlings and the decline of species such as the bald eagle. *Silent Spring* helped the modern environmental movement get its wings, and the movement in 1972 succeeded in having use of the chemical banned in the United States. (In one of history's curious footnotes, the big political push for a DDT ban came from Richard Nixon, looking to build bridges to the Left.)

Soon WHO and the U.S. Agency for International Development (USAID) cut out DDT from their programs and instead starting talking up bed nets as the way to prevent malaria. Bed nets do have some usefulness, but the mesh turns stifling in the heat, so many people foolishly but understandably will not use them. Besides, even the smallest gap or tear in a bed net allows in mosquitoes, and all it takes is one. In author-physician Michael Crichton's words, the de facto ban on DDT "has killed more people than Hitler." That's because trying to stop every human-stinging mosquito is a dead man's game. They will find a way in.

During George W. President Bush's first term, the United States contributed about $200 million per year to Africa's war on malaria. None of the money went for DDT spraying. In 2005 the president promised an additional $1.2 billion over five years in U.S. malarial funding. But that same year eminent malaria experts and public health specialists—including the former U.S. Navy surgeon general and the president of the Association of American Physicians and Surgeons—began to say loudly and publicly that the old money was, and the new money would be, misspent, unless allocations took into account two things we've learned in the three decades since DDT disappeared from the disease-fighting weapon rack.

First, Carson's concerns turned out to be overwrought. Lab experiments, in which captive birds ingested hundreds of times more DDT than their counterparts would encounter in the wild, did not determine that DDT thinned eggshells dangerously. Bird populations actually increased while DDT was in use. Nor is DDT carcinogenic to humans, as Carson claimed. Infants nursing when there's been heavy DDT spraying may gain weight a little more slowly than others, but that's a lot better than dying from malaria.

Second, government-to-government foreign aid has often been wasted, or worse. As Kenyan businessman Evans Konya put it: "There is so much corruption here that funds from overseas often go straight into the pockets of politicians. We must find a way to give aid . . . to the people on the ground." USAID has not been as bad as other organizations, according to Senate testimony in 2004 by Roger Bate, a resident scholar at the American Enterprise Institute, who stated, "The Agency would rather allocate its monies to U.S. organizations likely to waste a good portion of it but steal none, rather than local institutions that are in a better position to effectively use resources but are more vulnerable to instances of fraud and embezzlement."

Bate noted that USAID had not spent any money on DDT and very little even on less-efficient aids such as bed nets. Instead, it had concentrated on "paying Washington-based contractors to consult with local health ministers on policy matters, give advice on management issues, train selected administrators and health care workers, and help run basic health education programs." Millions in USAID antimalaria funds never leave the Washington area.

The politics of perpetual disaster spending lead to well-connected fat cats, thin Africans, and wasted opportunity. Bate described a typical USAID-funded project in Kenya that made "no effort to measure whether the project made any progress towards its goal (reduction of deaths and severe illness due to malaria)": "Instead [it] measured several objectives (five in this case) loosely related to its goal . . . revised downward its targets for some of those objectives after the mid-term report revealed unsatisfactory progress . . . failed to meet many of these objectives (even downwardly revised ones) . . . despite unimpressive results, the final evaluation gave the program a positive assessment."

Some Africans and some Americans have refused to give in. Zambia, for example, went ahead and used indoor spraying of DDT in some areas over the objection of some environmentalists; the result was a 75 percent drop in cases and deaths over two years. In the United States, the "Kill Malarial Mosquitoes Now" coalition that arose in 2005 included not only medical experts but also the national chairman of the Congress of Racial Equality, the president of the National Black Chamber of Commerce, and a co-founder of Greenpeace.

Their joint statement was, "We will fight furiously for every human life now hanging in the balance as a function of current, myopic, errant and unconscionable U.S. malaria control policies." In December 2005 USAID announced that 25 percent of its antimalarial funds would go for DDT. That's a start—but the record of disaster relief, whether in response to sudden calamities like tsunamis or long-term plagues like malaria, offers many reasons to distrust any professions of altruism that come from the foreign aid establishment.

THE POLITICS OF INTERNATIONAL DISASTER

Many insiders have testified to corruption. Monique Maddy, author of *Learning to Love Africa* (Collins, 2004), wrote of the "endless parade of well-paid experts [who have] little or no incentive to bring a project to fruition." She said, "On the contrary, any project that ended, successful or not, would reduce the number of consulting contracts available to the large cadre of international experts dependent on the U.N. system for their livelihoods."

Maddy, born in Liberia and having U.N. staff experience in Indonesia, Angola, and the Central African Republic, wrote of U.N.-sponsored events that she attended in compounds and convention centers, where Dom Perignon and vintage French wines flowed not far from shantytowns where rice and beans would be a feast. She described the pleasure of being "an academic, a self-appointed guru of global poverty, reeling in millions of publicly funded dollars to collect and disseminate data and writing alarming reports that I know will never be read, let alone acted upon."

Even *New York Times* columnist Nicholas Kristof acknowledged this, writing in 2005, "The liberal approach to helping the poor is sometimes to sponsor a U.N. conference and give ringing speeches calling for changed laws and more international assistance. In contrast a standard conservative approach is to sponsor a missionary hospital or school." Kristof also noted, "Plenty of studies have shown that aid usually doesn't help people in insecure, corrupt or poorly governed nations. Indeed, aid can even do harm, by bidding up local exchange rates and hurting local manufacturers."

New York University professor William Easterly noted amid concerts for African aid in 2005: "It's great that so many are finally noticing the tragedy of Africa. But sadly, historical evidence says that the solutions offered by big plans are not so easy. From 1960 to 2003, we spent $568 billion (in today's dollars) to end poverty in Africa. Yet these efforts still did not lift Africa from misery and stagnation." He wrote that the big plans don't work because "they miss the critical elements of feedback and accountability."

Easterly offered as an example the United Nations Millennium Project's proposal for "everything from nitrogen-fixing leguminous trees to replenish the soil, to rainwater harvesting, to battery-charging stations, for, by my count, 449 interventions." He said, "Poor Africans have no market or democratic mechanisms to let planners in New York know which of the 449 interventions they need, whether they are satisfied with the results, or whether the goods ever arrived at all."

He pointed out that "the trees don't grow well in shade, they can proliferate as weeds and they can wind up competing for soil nutrients, especially in arid areas. . . . It's easy to decree a solution at the top, but it will never work without the detailed local knowledge at the bottom—which planners in New York cannot possibly process." Easterly recommended instead that those wanting to help emphasize small, concrete steps, "like water pipes and wells, school buildings and vaccinations—where individual contributions can be measured."

The great need is to break through the current politics of international disaster, which suggest salvation by big government-to-government programs, backed up by military intervention in emergencies. Let's look at how faith-based groups and entrepreneurial attitudes can make at least small improvements.

Chapter 14

RELIGIOUS ENTREPRENEURS

In the United States we have occasional disasters and then spend months dissecting failures to react as quickly as we might like. But what about a continent that seems to suffer one disaster after another so that they all blend together, and it's hard to remember when life was not calamitous? Africans have lurched from disaster to disaster for centuries, as warring tribes—then Arab raiders and Europeans—enslaved millions. Later, colonial administrators and the native dictators that replaced them deprived most Africans of self-rule. And always, always malarial mosquitoes flew, sometimes causing death and frequently sapping the energy of those who survived.

The malaria disaster is easy to assist in one sense, though, since Africans are pleading for the tools that will help them to deal with it. When a disaster has a technological fix, we're already halfway toward success. But when a disaster emerges from deeply rooted cultural habits and religious gaps, the problem is much further away from solution. On July 2, 2005, hundreds of millions watched the Live8 concerts, which featured U2, Sting, Pink Floyd, REM, Elton John, Paul McCartney, and others singing their hearts out as part of the "End Poverty Now" campaign, sending the message that what Africa needed was more money. If only it were that easy.

Let's look at three examples of what American religious groups are doing to deal with a disaster without a technological fix: the spread of AIDS. Fewer than one of a hundred U.S. adults is HIV-positive, but probably one of five adults in sub-Saharan Africa is, and the macabre statistic may head even higher. Historically, epidemics have tended to kill the very young and the very old, but AIDS is different: those ages twenty to forty are most affected, which means that so far more than twelve million African children have been orphaned because of AIDS. Sometimes grandparents are able to care for these kids; sometimes twelve-year-olds care for their younger siblings; sometimes no one cares.

THE LOSKOP CONCERT

Just before the big-name acts went on stage in 2005, a different concert was held thousands of miles south in a cold, dimly lit room in the Zulu village of Loskop, four hours east of Johannesburg. There, eight boys and girls ages thirteen to eighteen stood in a circle and sang lines from a Ladysmith Black Mombazo song now popular across South Africa: "AIDS killed my father, AIDS killed my mother, AIDS is killing Africa." One singer ran his finger across his throat. Others stomped their feet on the cement floor. Then Rob Smith, the forty-seven-year-old, wispy-bearded head of the Agathos Foundation—*agathos* is Greek for "good"—told the eight about the "need to talk about sex." He said, "We need to talk about it openly so we can see what Jesus says about sex and about our bodies. Then we can relate that to the AIDS crisis."

The AIDS crisis affects Africa more than by its death count. UNICEF reports that two-thirds of rural orphans and one-third of urban ones are not enrolled in school. The World Bank reports high levels of malnutrition and stunted growth among half of South Africa's children. Many children survive by working long hours, sometimes in prostitution. But the thirty-two AIDS orphans on the dusty Agathos property in Loskop, along the Tugela River, are surviving, and Smith was trying to teach them not to throw their lives away. Wearing a T-shirt showing a tree planted by streams of water, he read to them the Ten Commandments, emphasizing "Do not commit adultery" and "Do not steal," and told them of predictions that "90 percent of you will be dead by the age of thirty."

Smith put his arm around one girl, said, "We're going to pretend that she's HIV-positive," and asked her to speak to three others. Giggling, she complied. Those three then spoke to the others. "That is how AIDS spreads," he said, explaining that he wasn't describing the literal spread of disease but was noting the ease with which cases could multiply. He contrasted that rapid multiplication with Christ's emphasis on sex only within marriage to one other person. He then pushed for feedback: "Tell me how AIDS gets spread." Bonga, the oldest teen present at age eighteen, made a comment in Zulu that set all the children laughing. He was trash talking about oral sex, but Smith pushed, "How many of you have heard at school or at the clinic that you must have protected sex?"

They all knew what he meant. A sign on the door of the nearby medical clinic offers free condoms, and that day representatives of an international organization had shown up in their Land Rover to make sure their doctrine was being taught. But Smith insisted: "The Bible says sex with the person you marry is the only protected sex. . . . If we have sex with someone who's not our wife or our husband, we're stealing from someone." The teens were silent. Smith pressed his point: "We prevent getting AIDS by abstaining from sex until we are married. God designed sex for marriage. . . . Those who are married know that sex is best when it's with one person for the rest of your life. God's design is always best for us. Right now, young men are sleeping with three, four, five girlfriends. That's why we have all these funerals."

Bonga wasn't buying. "Black people are not the same as white people," he said. "Black people do not abstain." Smith responded, "I understand that the Zulu people like to say they do things differently. But this is not about what Rob thinks, nor about what the white man thinks. This is about what God thinks. If you reject this, you're not rejecting man, but God." Bonga continued to insist: "We have sex before marriage." Smith shot back, "But Bonga can get AIDS and die." The debate has no resolution that night or in the months ahead, because the difference was not only about sex but about short-term versus long-term thinking, and about satisfying impulses versus building a different kind of life and society.

Rob Smith's Loskop program began in 2004 in a neighborhood called Injesuthi, which is Zulu for "the dog is satisfied." The site didn't use to satisfy anyone except the drunks who slept in shacks there, but the Agathos Foundation took out a thirty-year lease on the acreage for about $150 per month. The property now boasts a kitchen/dining room building, a structure with rooms for visitors, and apartments—typically two rooms, six bunks—for caretakers and children. The cement block and wood-frame and stucco buildings are cold from June through August, during southern hemisphere winter, for there is no central heating and, in many rooms, no heat at all.

The willingness to be cold, though, gives credibility to Smith's teaching that the way to fight everyday disaster is to work hard and be willing to make sacrifices. He says volunteers from America are sending a loud message by living and eating with the thirty-two children, lining up for showers just as they do, and not shoving to the front or having separate toilets. Missionary David Livingstone insisted 150 years ago that Africa needed two things—"Christianity and commerce"—and Smith sends the same dual message.

He is particularly insisting on teaching work habits. Children at the orphanage have chores that require effort but offer rewards. In the afternoon they put on rubber gloves to pick up garbage, with the incentive of being able to blow up those gloves into balloons when work is done. The children have also seen that two bicycles held in common for their use soon had broken chains and battered appearances: that was a lesson in how property that isn't owned is soon property that is broken or lost, since no one has much personal stake in maintaining it. The village of Loskop itself provides further evidence of ownership's importance, since a close-by, government-provided community center now has broken windows and is rarely used.

Smith has to battle the irresponsibility promoted by British colonialism, which brought some economic upgrades but a clear psychological down-grade, since the implicit message was that Africans were addlepated children. At this point helping many South Africans to move beyond dependency requires patience. When a bathroom door was off its hinges, Smith observed that he "could fix it in three minutes, but what good would that do?" He said, "People have to learn to fix things themselves." He was patient, and at the end of the day the door was fixed. His goal is to have a working farm where African teens would learn agricultural techniques they could then apply. He also casts a sadly realistic eye on business opportunities such as coffin mak-ing, likely to be a growth industry over the next decade.

If coffin making is not to be the major business in Africa, individual behavior must change along the lines Smith proposed to Bonga. Here's where the opportunity for Africans to recover from disaster parallels that of New Orleans residents: they can change most readily by following the Bible, and as in post-Katrina America, Christian groups are willing to help.

AFRICAN AID OR A NEW BUILDING?

Another example of how to fight African disaster emerged from a decision made in the mid-1990s by the members of Damascus Wesleyan Church in Damascus, Maryland, just north of Washington, D.C. The church had a small sanctuary and a growing congregation so that the congregation had to divide into two camps with separate services. Most people didn't like doing that, especially since the sanctuary wasn't even big enough for the second group, which had to meet in a local school.

Many churches would have raised funds for a new building. But when church members and associates donated and pledged $287,000 in a spe-cial offering one Sunday, it went to purchase a ninety-nine-year-lease on ten thousand acres in Senkobo, Zambia. The land came with a beautiful farmhouse, twenty-seven hundred fruit trees, cattle and other animals, four deep wells, three dams, a tobacco-curing barn that could be turned into apartments, and other farm buildings that could become orphanages and classrooms.

Because of that church decision, and the volunteers who inspired it and then moved to Africa, this part of the vast bush country now benefits from:

- an elementary school with three hundred students and five teachers, all men, who receive $120 to $150 per month from Sons of Thunder, the Christian nonprofit organization founded by Damascus church members.

- an orphanage to which motherless children close to death are brought; one, named Hope, was born two months prematurely and weighed less than two pounds when she arrived. She survived, as have thirty-four others in the home, with the oldest not yet four years old. Most of the mothers died of AIDS.

- teams of volunteers who pay for the opportunity to come for two weeks to three months and help with Sunday worship at four village churches and daily activities.

- a three-year course in Bible study and improved farming techniques that is already changing surrounding villages spiritually and physically. In the agricultural/Bible program, each family receives for three years twenty-five acres (with a water source, oxen, and a plow) of the ten-thousand-acre spread. Except during peak planting and harvesting periods, the men study the Bible from 9:00 a.m. to 3:00 p.m., three days a week.

- two- and three-bedroom homes for teachers and students that cost between $7,000 and $8,000 to build.

Another result became evident on a glorious day in June 2005, in the Zambian bush country, as thirty-nine Africans standing with four Americans on the back of a Mitsubishi flatbed truck (with one hundred fifty thousand miles on it) sang of their faith in Christ: "He is not number eight. He is not number six. He is number one." Standing behind the cab was like being at the prow of a ship with the wind blowing hard, and dirt roads tough on truck suspensions taking the place of waves. The truck bounced past mud huts with thatched roofs and darted between short, moisture-starved trees, as passengers ducked and watched for thorns (like fishhooks) that have an African name translated "Where do you think you were going?"

Adults and children in village after village greeted standees on the flatbed truck with friendly waves, and many dozens of smiling children ran after it, as in a Rocky movie. Zambians are friendly toward Americans, Jerry Beall, a former Damascus pastor who now spends much of his time in Africa, said, because "they see we're here to give and not take." (Add, don't subtract.) Truck standees got off at thatch-covered huts and greeted one another with formal words—"How are you doing, my brother?"—and informal hugs.

Megahuts housed churches with bricks as seats, which were filled with men on one side clapping and women on the other side, some nursing babies, dressed in their wraparound best. Hymns and spiritual songs wafted over the still air, with men's and women's quartets and quintets often leading the singing and showing off dance steps like those of the Temptations, their elegance marred only by pressure to get an awkward American male to join in—with friendly laughter overcoming politeness when he did.

The enthusiasm is unsurprising, given the alternative in African tradition. Traditionally in Zambia, omens of disaster are everywhere: for example, if an owl lights on a tree near a person's house, it means that someone in the family will die or be very sick. Zambians often believe that the spirits of ancestors inhabit the blossoms of the mighty baobab tree, and that a lion will eat anyone who plucks a flower from it. Damascus church member Mike Jones, who grew up on a North Carolina farm and now lives in Zambia teaching Africans how to improve agricultural productivity, calls the old ways "a fear-based culture."

With witch doctors still active in the Zambian bush country, it's often hard to leave such fears behind. Babies traditionally wear around their necks little charms that purportedly protect them from disaster. Beall, reports, "When we get ready to dedicate a baby to Christ, we ask for the charm. It's a real challenge: the mothers stand there with a life-and-death choice they have to make, and you can see on their faces the concern."

That's the choice much of Africa must make: between a fear-based animism and a faith in God who loves but also commands a way to stop the onslaught of AIDS. Witch doctors sometimes spread AIDS by telling a sick man that if he sleeps with a virgin, he'll be cured. Christians tell men and women that if they wait until marriage to have sex, they and their culture will progress. The challenge is great. One afternoon Beall climbed a Zambian hill to spend some time thinking about what his Maryland church gave up by investing in Africa. He looked around at land being farmed, watched some of the children playing between the school and the orphanage, and said, "See how much more we got."

AFRICAN AID OR AIR CONDITIONING?

Other American religious groups are also trying to become a blessing to entire African communities. A third example of how to respond to African disaster is on display inside the soft green walls of the Children of Zion orphanage in Katima Mulilo, Namibia. The home, built under a grove of shade trees along the Zambezi River, stands out against the blue of the sky and the river, the splash of scarlet from a bougainvillea climbing a fence, and the sandy soil. It's a pretty sight, but there's nothing pretty about the backgrounds of the fifty-two children within. Most have lost at least one parent to AIDS. Several—including one boy who had been living in a tire—were rescued from slavery. Two deaf boys had lived on the streets. Eleven children are known to carry the HIV virus.

The home exists because a Maryland pastor and church decided that children's lives were a higher priority than air conditioning. Children of Zion grew from the vision of Mount Zion, an evangelical United Methodist Church just north of Baltimore. One member, Benedict Schwartz, wanted to save some AIDS orphans in Africa, and he reminded his fellow trustees of a promise made by pastor Craig McLaughlin: the sanctuary would get air conditioning only after the congregation built a church in Africa. The church came up with the money, and from there, amazingly, everything—personnel, permits, property, governmental approvals, construction—went right. The orphanage opened in 2003 and now provides food, shelter, medical care, clothing, and schooling for the children at a cost of about $11,000 per month.

Eighty percent of Americans believe that money sent via government or big organizations won't get to the people most in need, but members of Mount Zion travel to Namibia to volunteer at the children's home and then return home to tell the congregation about what happens during a typical day there:

- Early in the morning, all the children (except the very youngest) go to their daily farm chores. The job of eleven-year-old Albert, the formerly enslaved boy who had lived in a tire, is to milk a goat—but yesterday he forgot to take in the milk. Today he discovers the spoilage and wants to cover it up by dumping the new milk on top of it. Another boy says he should ask someone, and—filled with fear about the consequences of honesty—Albert agrees to do so. He receives an admonition about responsibility but also praise for telling the truth.

- Classes begin after breakfast. Many of the kids had never been to school before coming to the home because they couldn't afford the fees (five dollars per term) or uniforms (the same amount). All classes are in English, and, in volunteer teacher Jaimie Bugaski's classroom, fourteen children crowd around two tables to study the difference between possessive and personal pronouns. When the teaching turns to geography, one boy, Martin, can name all seven continents and all four oceans.

- After lunch, another volunteer teacher, Lydia Alder, sits on the sandy ground outside the home while two almost-teenage girls painstakingly plait her long, blond hair into tiny braids. They've been working on it during recess and free time for several days. The three- and four-year-olds try to braid another volunteer's hair. Since they haven't yet mastered braiding, they twist and tug at it, managing to tie some of it in knots.

- At midafternoon, an African vet wearing a lab coat cuts into a goat that died from unknown causes. He suspects tick fever. Older children stare as the vet skins and beheads the animal, draping the skin over a wheelbarrow and painstakingly explaining his actions. An assistant sorts through the pile of guts to produce a stomach, kidneys, heart, and intestines. The vet cuts open each organ, using his scalpel to point out signs of disease.

- Late in the afternoon, Mark Chiyuka, a Namibian auto mechanic, teaches bicycle repair to five boys in the shade near a sandy drive. On a tarp are a few bicycle frames, flat tires, and a box of parts. Each afternoon the boys come and learn how to straighten fenders, adjust seats, tighten chains, and repair wheels. Chiyuka and the boys work side by side. He often pauses from his own work to answer their questions and resolve disputes. When two boys start to fight over a wrench, he says, "Don't fight. Why should you fight?"

Outside the orphanage are Namibia government billboards advocating condom use to fight AIDS. Outside are other indicators of Africa's ongoing disasters: poverty, disease, and fatalism. Inside the children have hope. Not a bad substitute for air conditioning a Maryland sanctuary.

Chapter 15

THE NEED FOR CIVIL SOCIETY

Paul Theroux, in *Dark Star Safari* (Houghton Mifflin, 2003), writes about traveling by cattle truck through northern Kenya and being ambushed by bandits. "I don't want to die," he told the African with him, who responded, "They don't want your life, bwana. They want your shoes." That thought became a centerpiece of Theroux's book: "Many times after that, in my meandering through Africa, I mumbled these words, an epitaph of underdevelopment, desperation in a single sentence. What use is your life to them? It is nothing. But your shoes—ah, they are a different matter."

One of *Dark Star Safari*'s recurring themes is the witting or unwitting damage done to Africa by Western charities and other aid programs. "Agents of virtue" appear and reappear, whizzing by in their white Land Rovers, full of noble intentions and rarely questioning whether their aid is helping or hurting its recipients. Theroux describes aid workers staying in the best hotels, driving luxury vehicles, talking on cell phones, listening to their CDs, and refusing to give lifts to stranded travelers. Their aid allows African leaders to stay in power, indifferent to the needs of their people, and turns those people into "beggars and whiners."

Theroux was a Peace Corps teacher from 1963 to 1965 in Malawi and a regular English teacher there for three more years. When he returned four decades later, he expected some improvement, but Africans told him that life was worse. He discovered that international aid has helped to "destroy initiative and create a sense of entitlement" and reported how a Malawi government minister had "stolen the entire education budget of millions of dollars."

Those stories are common, but they do not represent the worst type of political disaster that can occur. Stealing the education budget is not as bad as establishing a totalitarian educational system that force-feeds students governmental propaganda. Taking some property unjustly is not as bad as mandating a communist system that allows no significant property in private hands. A strict wall of separation between church and state can be counterproductive, but it's not as bad as having the state declare all church services illegal unless they are held by governmental consent and under governmental supervision.

The worst twentieth-century disasters were not natural but unnatural, caused by governments: state-caused famines in the Ukraine and in Ethiopia, Mao's murderous Great Leap Forward, Pol Pot's killing of one-third of Cambodia. This chapter provides two case studies showing the importance of civil society, particularly religious and independent educational institutions, in two Latin American countries. First, we'll examine how Chile resurrected itself from a three-year attempt to establish a Communist dictatorship and the fifteen years of military control that followed. Then we'll see how church institutions in Cuba are helping to relieve people from total dependence on a government that wants to be totalitarian.

POLITICAL DISASTER

The Chile story begins with the presidential election of 1970, in which Marxist Salvador Allende received 36 percent of the vote in a three-way race and became president. His opponents were not overly alarmed: Allende lived in the affluent Providencia section of Santiago with his wife and three daughters; owned a seashore villa across from the yacht club in an expensive summer resort; owned an estate in the foothills of the Andes where he housed his longtime mistress; and drank a lot of Scotch whisky, particularly the expensive Chivas Regal. So to some he seemed domesticated.

Except for inflation, the economic indices were good as Allende took power. Copper prices were strong and unemployment was about 3 percent. Allende initially seized some foreign firms, took over banks, and encouraged local workers to seize farms by force, with farm owners and their families forced out onto the road. Allende stated that his goal was "to expropriate the means of production." He said, "Our objective is total, scientific, Marxist socialism," but most Chileans thought he practiced junk science. Food output fell sharply, and thousands of Chilean women marched in the streets of Santiago, banging on empty pots and pans to dramatize the growth of shortages and skyrocketing prices.

Allende imposed a state of emergency that allowed him to censor newspapers, close radio stations, and ban demonstrations. He soon announced that the government would be in charge of all food distribution and would establish a single nationwide curriculum, modeled on East Germany's, with compulsory courses on Marxism. As the economy shrank while government spending increased, currency printing presses worked overtime and inflation leaped. The consumer price index, which stood at 100 when Allende became president, was at 942 three years later. Allende imposed food rationing and took shipments from Cuba and other Communist countries of enough machine guns, bazookas, mortars, antitank guns, carbines, automatic pistols, ammunition, and explosives to equip a militia of over fifteen thousand committed to seizing factories and killing opponents.

The number of opponents grew. Sixty thousand truck owners, one hundred ten thousand bus and taxi drivers, and four hundred fourty thousand shopkeepers went on strike in July and August 1973, calling for Allende to resign. Conservatives sharpened their criticism, and Patricio Alwyn, leader of the moderate party, told the *Washington Post* that if he had to decide between "a Marxist dictatorship and a dictatorship of the military, I would choose the second." Chile's legislature voted almost two-to-one that Allende "from the very beginning has persisted in pursuing total power, with the obvious purpose of submitting everyone to the strictest economic and political control of the State, and implanting thereby a totalitarian system."

The legislature pointedly reminded military leaders of their oaths to uphold the constitution and asked them to take steps to "channel government action along legal paths and thereby assure the constitutional order of our country." They said, "If they do these things, the [military leaders] will perform a valuable service for the Republic." When Allende refused to resign, the military, on September 11, 1973, overthrew his regime and offered an airplane to take him and his family to the foreign destination of his choice. When he refused, soldiers assaulted the presidential palace, and Allende shot himself with an AK-47 that Fidel Castro had given him.

Some three thousand people died in scattered fighting over the next several months. That was far different from the two million who would be killed in Cambodia later in the decade, but still a disaster that, along with destroying many families, has roiled Chilean politics ever since. The military stayed in power for the next fifteen years, until in a 1988 referendum 54 percent of Chileans voted to have elections the following year. The following year a moderate became president. Now, although wall drawings of Allende and hammer-and-sickle Communist Party posters can still be seen on the outskirts of Santiago, much of the country has recovered politically from revolution and counterrevolution.

CHILEAN COMPASSIONATE CONSERVATISM

And yet poverty mixes with economic improvement: in one neighborhood old tires and rusting oil drums sit beside the main street under signs for Blockbuster videos and Nintendo Play Stations, with horse-drawn carts (horses for work, not for show) plodding down dirt roads. The hope for Chile's long-term recovery from disaster is the same odd couple that David Livingstone spoke of as the hope for Africa: Christianity and commerce.

That's because it's vital to disprove Allende's faith that workers could advance only through class warfare.

One of many attempts at disproof is the Liceo Industrial Italia, a private high school for five hundred fifty male students in a poor area of Santiago. Italia provides a liberal arts education but prepares graduates for jobs as electricians, welders, draftsmen, designers, and so on. Inside a renovated building with wood-colored tiles and pastel yellow and blue pillars, classrooms are warm and teachers proceed from a Christian worldview. Science teacher Fernando Jorquera noted, "We show the hypotheses about the beginning of the world, such as evolution, but we teach the creation. Life started with God." Italia's underlying theory is that if people work hard at their trades, receive the fruits of their labors, and see themselves as part of God's plan, they will not be susceptible to the demagoguery of the left, and there will be no need to choose between one type of dictatorship and another.

Another private school for poor children, the Colegio San Joaquín (CSJ), is a K-12 that educates many students from hard family pasts. Only about one-fourth live with both birth parents, and their average family income is about $200 per month obtained through construction, selling vegetables, or working in homes or at restaurants. The children, though, are likely to have better lives economically. In the computer room at 5:00 p.m. one day, older students were searching Web sites to learn about different occupations and were preparing PowerPoint presentations for classmates about what they found. Some will receive diplomas in accounting, others in computing, and about one in seven will go on to university study for other occupations.

CSJ is financed by individual donations and contributions, by corporations that garner a tax deduction for giving, and also by a per-student stipend from the national government, for which all schools, whether public or private, religious or not, are eligible. Nearly half of Chilean students attend private schools. CSJ has demonstrated both social improvement—fewer problems with drugs or pregnancy—and academic growth.

A third program, Fundación Miguel Kast, is helping with spiritual and economic advancement in the very poor community of Buin, located about twenty miles south of Santiago. It is a place where even intact families often have only seasonal work, harvesting grapes, apples, and peaches.

Housing is tight: in a typical old, two-family house, each family has a bed-room and shares a living/dining/cooking room containing a television, antiquated stove, and refrigerator.

The day I visited a Fundación building in Buin, though, 110 boys and girls ages six to fourteen were spending their after-school hours learning the Christian values exemplified by a sign in teacher Sylvia Tapia's office: *No digas Padre si cada dia no te compartas como hijo* ("Do not call Him Father if each day you do not act like His Son"). The Chilean government was paying most of the after-school program's cost and imposing no restrictions on religious content, since many Chileans, as Mrs. Tapia said, consider religious development with biblical values *muy importante*.

The Fundación also was helping crowded families get new houses. One recently built, for the family of a seasonal farm worker with two children, has a cozy kitchen, living/dining room, and bathroom on the first floor, and two bedrooms upstairs. It cost $6,000, with businesses contributing raw materials and lawyers volunteering to handle the paperwork to assure property rights. This aid is the best defense against a future Allende encour-aging roving bands to seize land by force. In Chile, as in other South American countries, many people squat on land without a clear legal trail, but that leaves them without a ready source of capital or a defense against arbitrary government power. As Fundación executive director Cecilia Milevcic explained, Christian education, plus the establishment of prop-erty rights, leads people to embrace "values from the Bible, such as being honest instead of stealing, such as thinking about the future."

On a national scale, Jose Pinera, an economist who headed Chile's priva-tization of social security two decades ago, sees the same hope for a society "grounded in Christian values, the free market, and personal responsibility." A good government, he added, does not "allow people to starve, but it also requires an able-bodied man to work, save, and be responsible." He said, "We say, 'You will not smoke marijuana all day long,' and we emphasize eco-nomic growth so that poor people who are very disciplined and honest can go up the ladder." Pinera pulled from under his blue shirt a cross that he wears on a thin chain around his neck and said, "This is one thing that does not change. This makes the difference."

Communist ideas of social change emphasize working million by million from the top down: seize control of government and control schools and media so that people receive a standard message day after day; those people, plastic by nature, will conform to the new way. That approach led to disaster and counterdisaster, but more Chileans now appear to be emphasizing Christian social change that comes one person at a time from the inside out—one person, one family, one business at a time. Add up the individual changes and the result is a changed culture in which groups interact peacefully with one another rather than creating disasters by blasting those perceived as getting in the way.

THE CUBAN ALTERNATIVE

Had Allende been able to stay in power, Chileans would probably be going through the travail Cubans have had for nearly a half century, and one that will not be over when Fidel Castro dies. Havana priest Eduardo Pini offered, in 2004, the prediction that many are making: a post-Communist Cuba will include much "bloodshed, since now we have much hatred," he said. "Families have been destroyed by informants, so we have many suspended vendettas waiting to happen. We will have at first lots of blood in the streets."

That may happen if the only reply to decades of dictatorship is vengeance. Early in 2006 dissidents, reformers, Marxist true believers, and generals, planning to become great capitalists in post-Castro Cuba, all awaited a fatal subtraction. Many were bicycling along in a peloton worthy of the Tour de France, watching one another nervously and wondering whether to try a breakaway that could work exquisitely well if the timing is right, but end in imprisonment or worse if the quickened pace is premature. Yet what if individuals and organizations could instead concentrate on a productive transition? After a disastrous half century of political oppression and economic collapse, could Cubans avoid the further disaster of a bloody civil war?

One expression common in Cuba, *Ni comen ni dejan comer* ("They don't eat, neither do they let others eat"), demonstrates that it may be difficult to avoid further disaster: a failing government is trying to keep people from helping others and themselves. In Cuba now, churches are ready and willing to do better than the government in helping the poor and particularly the elderly, but officially and ideologically the state is responsible for providing all social services. Officials turn down church requests to build homes for the elderly and even citizen attempts to organize the collection of rotting garbage. Such steps are indictments of government failure—and Cuba's Communist Party is desperately trying to avoid facing the truth.

Another expression, *No es facil* ("It's not easy"), signifies that every aspect of life—from gaining basic material sustenance, to traveling across town, to remaining psychologically relaxed when any neighbor or associate might be an informer—is difficult. Most Cubans have to break the law regularly by buying needed food on the black market, or by paying for medical care when the state health system fails them. Rationed food is insufficient, and only three groups of people—recipients of money from relatives in the United States, tourist industry workers, and prostitutes—can generally afford "luxuries" like extra coffee (the ration is enough to make four to five cups per month) or soap (one small bar is available per person per month, which is heaven for small boys but hard on others).

In a society long known for being child friendly, the milk shortage particularly distresses Cubans. When a baby is born, parents get a card that is supposed to entitle them to a quart of milk per week until the child is seven years old. But Cubans regularly say that some milk never shows up, other portions are watery, and the kind distributed to children ages three to six is of such low quality that many children have stomach problems. When children are sick, parents find that medicine is scarce and hospitals are unhygienic. At some hospitals the new tradition is BYOX—"Bring Your Own X-ray" film.

If the United States is a paperocracy, the Castro regime has turned Cuba into a "kleptocracy." We've seen in the United States that material resources given to addicted parents usually feed their addiction, not their children. Similarly any humanitarian aid sent to Cuba through official government channels or through government-controlled nongovernmental organizations (that oxymoron is standard in Havana) goes to strengthen the totalitarian apparatus. Once in a while material brought into the Port of Havana can get into the right hands, but the cost in bribes is high. Even if those offering charity choose to ignore the regime-strengthening effects, they still fail in their attempts, because kleptocracy swallows all: milk shipped in for children turns into ice cream for tourists.

So Cuba has suffered through a long disaster that is only growing more severe. Partly in response to that, many churches are once again growing. Of Cuba's eleven million people, probably five hundred thousand attend Roman Catholic mass at least weekly, and several million more feel some Catholic connection. The largest growth of biblical sensibility in recent years has been among Protestants, who now number between six hundred thousand and two million. Churches deal with a psychological disaster even greater than the material one. As one African resident of Havana observed, "People generally have learned to be two-faced, superfriendly on the outside but ready to stab you in the back if they need to in order to survive." Those who have been betrayed come to church looking for authenticity.

A precise number of Cuban churchgoers is hard to come by because fewer than two hundred thousand Cubans adhere to establishment denominations that make up the *Consejo de Iglesias*, the Cuban Council of Churches, which is a leftist body tightly connected to and directed by government authorities. The explosive growth has come in unregistered *casas cultos*, or house churches that grow despite harassment and persecution. Their leaders are the ones best able to lead Cuba out of its disaster.

RISK-TAKING CHRISTIANS

Among the nonestablishment leaders has been Leoncio Veguilla, president of the Baptist Convention of Western Cuba, who did hard labor in prison from 1965 to 1970 for not toeing the party line. He spent time in a forced labor camp, cutting sugar cane alongside criminals and other religious prisoners labeled by the government as "social scum." He looks back on that time as "very difficult, but an opportunity to preach the gospel to prisoners," many of whom became Christians. Today he is hoping for the opportunity to do more for the elderly. The government allows Baptists to run one home with room for thirty *ancianos*, but he hopes to expand that and open more.

Many local pastors like Efrain Paz have stepped up. Paz, an Assemblies of God minister who rides a 1963 Czech motorcycle, turned his backyard into a church sanctuary with room for eighty-four battered folding chairs, twelve white plastic porch chairs, twenty-eight wooden seats from a movie theater, and a pulpit. He wants to distribute medicine to those in need. He has already been threatened with prison for doing that, but it was hard to throw the pastor in jail for helping the sick when the state health service is so obviously failing. He's learned this lesson: "Officials say, 'You can't do it, can't do it, can't do it.' But if you've already done it and enough people like it, they may say, 'So be it.'"

Some women have formed independent social service agencies. Among them is Dulce L. Montalvan Diaz, director of the interdenominational *Ministerio de Ayuda a Necesitados y Ancianos* (help for the needy and the elderly), who works to distribute milk to children and meet other needs as well. From her office with cracked vinyl couches at the top of two flights of dark and narrow stairs, she tries to keep track of resources and needs on a "Frankenstein computer" that was constructed part by part from computers that died. She said, "I don't have a budget. I scrounge. . . . The need for medicine is great."

Some Catholic priests like Father Pini of the Orden de las Escuelas Pias distribute medicine and other material help to church members, even though state health officials threaten them. In Pini's case, Spanish friends donate the medicine, and trustworthy tourists from Barcelona bring it: "The needs of the people are so great that the political cost of shutting us down is too great for the government. . . . They don't facilitate, but they don't send police to shut us down—for the moment."

Representatives of some international groups like the Salvation Army still remain in Havana. Salvation Army captain Odilio Fernandez runs an old-age home there: at one prayer meeting, sixteen elderly women, bright-eyed and alert, and some holding Bibles, asked God for wisdom in using their time and for His mercy in the lives of each others' children and grandchildren. Thirty other aged men and women live there in dignity, with three to five to a room.

Fernandez noted that when he requested permission to open another home for the elderly in a vacant building that would have worked well for that purpose, the government said no. He said: "The government always says 'this far and no further.' If we had freedom we would open up elderly homes everywhere."

The projects of all five of these bold leaders have two elements in common: Christianity and charity. Or maybe they're one and the same, since the two have regularly gone together. Communists seek power and speak of love. Christians show love and, over time, defeat power—and that may happen in Cuba. Whether government officials are incompetent, corrupt, or hamstrung by regulations or paperocracy, the need when facing natural disasters in the United States or political disasters in Cuba is to establish and support institutions that can do the job. In Cuba, given its history of political disaster, this is a radical proposal. Centers of governance cannot merely supplement current institutions of governance, but need to lay the groundwork for supplanting them.

Cuban churches might even learn something from Vladimir Lenin's article "Letters from Afar . . . The First Stage of the First Revolution," written (and published by the newspaper *Pravda*) in March 1917, eight months before the Bolshevik seizure of power. Lenin wrote, "Side by side with this government . . . there has arisen the chief, unofficial, as yet undeveloped and comparatively weak workers' government . . . the Soviet of Workers' Deputies in Petrograd." Lenin called the Soviets "the embryo of a workers' government, the representative of the interests of the entire mass of the poor section of the population, i.e., of nine-tenths of the population, which is striving for peace, bread, and freedom."

Cuban Christians are standing Lenin on his head by building structures for health, education, and social welfare that run parallel to the failed institutions of Marxist autocracy. Christian organizations that now distribute medicine and milk are learning to take action outside government control; in essence, they are preparing for a democratic transition in Cuba, helping new centers of governance to emerge. Some Americans are helping by obtaining humanitarian visas and bringing in suitcases full of medicine or 120 pounds of powdered milk packets. Cuban Christians then distribute the medicine and milk, sometimes trucking it to eastern Cuba (where shortages are even greater than in Havana), and discreetly making home deliveries by bicycle.

This is all slow going, and it has to be, since such activity threatens Communist officials, but every suitcase full of medicine provides immediate help and also contributes to the building of civil society. Most Americans have learned not to send any aid that the Cuban government or its lapdog groups control. U.S. evangelical denominations, however, can push for permission to send material aid for the construction of homes for the elderly—evangelical after evangelical in Cuba sees that as a great need and a great opportunity—on a denomination-to-denomination basis. Other means of building up those who have stood up to Castro provide the greatest opportunity to end Cuba's long disaster, not with a bang but a kiss.

Part Six

DISASTERS TO COME

Economist Stephen Moore accurately noted, "These are the safest times ever to have lived on the earth." A useful book, *The Good Old Days— They Were Terrible!* (Random House, 1974), documents how most jobs now tend to be more interesting than plowing or assembly line work, how most of today's American poor have items that once were luxuries, how today's car emissions are far less noxious than yesterday's horse emissions, how rivers no longer contain untreated sewage, and so on.

ABC's John Stossel has complained: "We are always ranting about the latest horror. When I asked a class of grade-school students whether what they saw on TV made them feel safe, they said, 'No, no, no.' Many worried about being kidnapped. They keep on saying stuff like 'a kid got kidnapped.' . . . But the crime rate is the lowest it's been in more than fifteen years, and the Justice Department says there's been no increase in kidnapping." Not only children are worrying. On a normal morning a television viewer may see an ABC story about a potential avian flu outbreak in which millions could die; in the afternoon a CNN talk show concerning hurricanes, fires, and "the next great quake"; and in the evening a Fox program totaling up the money it will take to pay for disaster relief.

The Associated Press wire on January 2, 2006, had 126 stories containing the word *disaster*. Among the headlines were: "Miners Trapped in West Virginia Coal Mine"; "Firefighters Still Battling Blazes Across Texas"; "Floodwaters Kill Nearly 400 Sheep in Nevada"; "Winter Storm Moves South"; "Tornadoes Hit Parts of Eastern U.S."; and "Three Die as a Result of Heavy Rains, Swollen Rivers" in the Pacific Northwest. International headlines were: "Flooding Kills at Least 34 People in Central Indonesia"; "Rain, Snow Buffet Pakistan Quake Zone"; and "Roof Collapses at Ice Rink in Germany." And this is just one day.

This section looks at the disasters most likely to come—a California earthquake, nuclear terrorism, and a pandemic—but does not suggest that life is harder now than it was in other eras, nor that we should live in fear. Instead, we should realistically assess the dangers, do what we can to reduce the risk, and, in the end, rely on providence.

Chapter 16

EARTHQUAKES AND NUCLEAR TERRORISM

Late in 2005 the *National Journal* offered a long list of disaster possibilities and noted that we cannot rule out any of them. An earthquake, starting in the Pacific Ocean on the Cascadia fault west of Oregon and Washington, could push a wall of water onto the coastline, causing substantial damage and infrastructure failure. In the Atlantic a Canary Island landslide could trigger a tsunami slamming into the Eastern Seaboard. The West Coast tsunami probably occurs about every five hundred years, and an East Coast version is also unlikely, but they could happen.

As for other disasters, a major earthquake is likely in California sometime in the first half of this century, but so is a Midwest earthquake. The New Madrid quake two centuries ago did little damage because the population was small and buildings rare; an earthquake like it today would cause huge damage to Memphis and St. Louis. Flood possibilities also worry specialists in the Midwest and California.

Clearly the only thing we have to fear is not fear itself. Tornadoes are always possible in tornado alley, which stretches from Oklahoma to the Dallas–Fort Worth area. Chemical spills usually affect only a few people, but a giant one could create thousands of victims of toxic gas. Hurricanes like Katrina hit Miami twice in the twentieth century and New York once, so those cities should be prepared. Wildfires threaten western homes every year, although fatalities are far fewer than the twelve hundred who died in a Wisconsin wildfire in 1871.

Unlikely disasters include a still-unexplained 1886 earthquake in Charleston, South Carolina (which is not near a fault), that killed sixty people, and a gas explosion in Cleveland in 1944 that killed one hundred thirty. A ship loaded with fertilizer and ammunition exploded in a fireball and destroyed much of downtown Texas City, Texas, in 1947. The Chicago heat wave in 1995 led to about seven hundred fatalities. If we're looking for something else to worry about, we can contemplate the rupture of a tank of warm molasses in 1919 that sent two million gallons of stickiness into the streets of Boston. It sounds funny, but the wave of goo destroyed buildings and resulted in twenty-one deaths.

Federal judge Richard Posner also wants us to contemplate the possibility of a massive asteroid collision, abrupt climate changes, or even a catastrophic accident caused by unfettered scientific exploration (for example, a "strangelet" scenario in which hyperdense quarks produced in a physicist's lab compress the earth in seconds). It is useful to remember that when cataclysmic forces are unleashed, people go out the window along with guarantees —but we cannot live out every science-fiction movie plot, nor can we adequately prepare for every realistic possibility. We can, though, prepare ourselves to think ahead without fretting and to respond without panicking.

EARTHQUAKE PROBABILITIES

In that spirit we'll look first in this chapter at the most likely calamity to come. Many publications have noted the famous FEMA emergency training session in August 2001, where participants agreed on the three major disasters most likely to strike the United States: a New York terrorist attack, a massive hurricane hitting New Orleans, and a major California earthquake. Two of the three have occurred, and the third is likely: a U.S. Geological Survey working group in 2002 estimated a 62 percent probability of a Richter 6.7 or greater earthquake in the San Francisco Bay area by 2032.

Those numbers have produced scary stories with predictions, like this from the *Denver Post*, that the next Bay Area earthquake "will be much worse than 1906." Maybe. Rarely do we see explanations of why predicted percentages of likelihood vary so widely. For example, one forecast published by University of California–Davis researchers in the Proceedings of the National Academy of Sciences, late in 2005, gave the San Francisco area a 25 percent chance of being struck by a Richter 7.0 or greater earthquake in the next twenty years, a 50 percent chance in the next forty-five years, and a 75 percent chance in the next eighty years.

To interpret such figures we need to know three things about earthquakes. The first is—no surprise—they are very powerful. A Richter 5.0 yields as much energy as the Nagasaki atomic bomb. A Richter 7.0 yields as much energy as the largest thermonuclear weapon ever made. The Pakistan earthquake in 2005 was a 7.6; the 1906 San Francisco earthquake is estimated to have been an 8.0; and the Indian Ocean earthquake that caused the terrible tsunami in 2004 was a 9.0.

The second is that, as with a bomb, the distance from its epicenter to major cities is crucial in determining the amount of damage it does. The California earthquake during the 1989 World Series was a 6.9 that would have been more devastating had the epicenter been right under San Francisco, but it was sixty miles away. Still the earthquake killed sixty-three and created $10 billion of damage, but that was merciful compared to the Richter-similar but closer-in one that struck Kobe, Japan, six years later, killing sixty-five hundred people and causing at least $150 billion in damage.

The third understanding that we need is of the Richter scale, because the difference between a Richter 6.7 earthquake (probable in San Francisco by 2032) and a 7.0 (improbable) is far greater than it appears. The Richter scale is logarithmic, which means that the seismic waves of a magnitude 7.0 earthquake are ten times greater than those of a 6.0, and that the energy released (proportional to the square root of the cube of the amplitude) is thirty-one times greater. Or, to put it simply, a 7.0 is about eleven times more powerful than a 6.7.

This all means that the results of a major earthquake in northern California could vary from those of a normal hurricane to those far worse than anything New Orleans saw. The common nightmare scenario has an equivalent of a massive nuclear weapon going off in the San Andreas Fault, which runs beneath San Francisco. Another vision of horror predicts a close epicenter, 6.9-or-greater quake striking Oakland or Berkeley; one million people live over the Hayward Fault, which runs right underneath the University of California football stadium.

The U.S. Geological Survey pegged the severe Hayward Fault possibility at only 8.5 percent during the next thirty years, so throughout the length of his career an East Bay politician playing Russian roulette with those odds is holding two six-shooters with a bullet in only one of the chambers; the odds of escaping disaster during a particular four-year term of office are very good. The same odds lead many to go without earthquake insurance: premiums run $1,000 to $2,000 per year, and only 15 percent of California homeowners carry it, with many apparently assuming that FEMA will bail them out if "the big one" does hit.

A close 6.9 earthquake would create so much destruction that 360,000 people would most likely become homeless, according to the Association of Bay Area Governments. That figure could be cut substantially if homeowners bolted their houses to their foundations, but since few do, William Lettis of the U.S. Geological Survey working group said simply, "Certain communities in the East Bay have the potential to become ghost towns."

Whether a 6.9 or higher earthquake occurred in the San Andreas Fault or the Hayward, timing would also be important. If it came during rush hour, thousands of subway riders could die in the BART Transbay Tube. BART subway stations and underground garages would be flooded. The easternmost part of the Bay Bridge, which lost part of its upper deck in the 1989 earthquake, stands in deep mud and would probably collapse. If the earthquake happened during the workday, a half million commuters would be stranded and homeless in San Francisco for at least several days.

Hundreds of nonreinforced concrete office buildings would pancake, crushing all within.

AFTER THE EARTHQUAKE

San Francisco's city plan rightly places a lot of responsibility on city emergency, police, and fire workers. However, most of them cannot afford to live in the city that they are sworn to protect, so they often reside across the Bay Bridge. If the earthquake happened when they were off duty, they would most likely have no way to report to work. A San Francisco civil grand jury reported in 2003 that "first responders" were not ready to respond.

The jury also noted that government officials were producing lots of plans but even more confusion. They determined that San Francisco's situation was much like that of New Orleans when Katrina hit: the report stated that agencies were updating their plans without distributing new versions to other agencies and the public, so that agencies were likely to act at cross-purposes. Furthermore, guidelines seemed often intentionally vague, so that agencies would be protected against lawsuits that would be filed if the agencies failed. Again, paper ruled.

In 2006 San Francisco was facing a paperocracy that made leadership more difficult than it was a century before. When the San Francisco earthquake in 1906 threatened to turn what was then the eighth largest American city into a carnival of looting, Frederick Funston—in charge of the San Francisco army garrison—ordered every available soldier to march to City Hall in full battle dress. Two hours later, two companies presented themselves to the mayor, who then issued an order saying that looters would be shot.

But not even Funston could fix the other emergency likely to develop following an earthquake: flooding. The levees of northern California are not as famous as those of New Orleans, but they are even more fragile. The eleven hundred miles of levees defend farmland within the Sacramento–San Joaquin Delta, a sixteen-hundred-square-mile plain that is up to thirty feet below sea level. It's where San Francisco Bay, the Sacramento River, and four other rivers come together. The area is so vulnerable that a massive storm or earthquake could collapse the levees and turn the area with its thousands of homes into a lake.

The consequences would reach far beyond the immediate victims: the brackish water rushing in after levee failure would contaminate the drinking water for twenty-two million Californians and the irrigation supply for five million acres of the Central Valley, America's leading agricultural producer. The levees, originally built by a nineteenth-century, largely Chinese labor force, are for the most part poorly built earthen dams that are already taxed to their capacity (and sometimes beyond). Southern California has six months of water reserves, but it would take longer than that to remove saltwater that would have rushed over collapsed levees.

As in New Orleans, maintenance of the levees is erratic. About one-third is maintained by state and federal agencies, but the rest fall under the authority of numerous delta reclamation districts. Meanwhile more homes are foolishly being built in flood-prone areas; for example, the delta town of Lathrop plans to grow from twelve thousand to eighty thousand residents over the next quarter century, with most new residents living in a master-planned community.

Southern California's water supply could be protected by building a canal to bring water from the Sacramento River to the southern part of the state without having to send it through the readily flooded Delta. But Californians, in 1982, voted not to spend money on building the Peripheral Canal, expecting the federal government to pay for it. "Moral hazard" struck again, and a quarter of a century later the pipeline is not built.

Although northern California receives most of the earthquake attention, researchers at the Southern California Earthquake Center speak of an 80 to 90 percent chance that a temblor of 7.0 or greater magnitude will strike Southern California before 2024. Some preparations have been made: almost all of the two thousand one hundred freeway overpasses that needed reinforcement have had it. Most at risk throughout California are school buildings: a report in 2001 found that of nearly ten thousand brick and concrete school buildings constructed before a 1978 state building code upgrade, 7,537 (78 percent) were "not expected to perform well in future earthquakes," and 1,229 of those buildings were within about a mile of an active fault.

State officials did not divulge names of the specific schools at risk, although school districts were allowed to request this information. Most have not, perhaps in the belief that districts are not legally liable if a disaster occurs and officials are ignorant. Or perhaps politicians are once again playing the percentages: if children are in school seven hours per day over 180 days of the year, and if an earthquake does occur and buildings collapse, there's only a one-in-seven chance that children will be buried in the rubble. Gambling with lives in that way seems foolhardy, but many people have short memories and even shorter perspectives on events yet unseen.

Concern about levees folding under natural pressures can also lead to reflection on how easily they could be destroyed with unnatural ones. Katrina gave some advance notice, although the available time was not always used well, but a terrorist who explodes a levee using a truck bomb is unlikely to send engraved invitations. Of course terrorists may not have to rely on blowing up levees; some may be able to steal nuclear bombs, smuggle them into the United States, and multiply the 9/11 killings a hundredfold.

NUCLEAR TERRORISM

In 2004 just about the only similar answer George W. Bush and John Kerry gave in their first presidential debate came when they were asked to define the "single most serious threat to American national security." Both answered, "Nuclear terrorism." In 2005 President Bush, Vice President Dick Cheney, and Homeland Security secretaries Tom Ridge and Michael Chertoff all said or implied the same.

As with earthquakes, some experts have assigned percentages of likelihood. Graham Allison, the Kennedy school dean and author of *Nuclear Terrorism*, says a nuclear attack on U.S. soil within the next ten years is probable. Former secretary of defense William Perry put the odds for an attack by 2010 at 50-50. Other experts, according to a survey by Senator Richard Lugar, put the likelihood over the next ten years at only 30 percent. CIA director Porter Goss told the Senate Intelligence Committee, in 2005, that enough nuclear material to make a bomb was missing from Russia, and that he had no idea where it was. He and others are not professional fear mongers, but they're concerned for three reasons: material, means, and motive.

Material: Nine countries—the United States, Russia, China, the United Kingdom, France, Israel, India, Pakistan, and North Korea—have nuclear weapons, and Iran is knocking on the door. Forty countries have among them about one hundred thirty nuclear research reactors, about one-fifth of which have enough highly enriched uranium (HEU) for one or more nuclear bombs. The number of existing nuclear weapons is probably around thirty thousand, with enough HEU and plutonium stockpiled for two hundred forty thousand more.

Leaders of North Korea and Iran sympathize with terrorist groups. Pakistani politics are brittle. Some of Russia's ten thousand nuclear warheads, along with its fissile material for thirty thousand more, could be stolen or sold for rubles, and it is now easy to get material across its porous borders. Over the past fifteen years the Russians have reported hundreds of thefts of nuclear material, generally unrefined and therefore not immediately weapon usable. Incidents that stand out include a plot in 1998 by nuclear facility employees to smuggle out forty pounds of HEU for black market sale, and the attempt in 2003 of Alexander Tyulyakov, deputy director of the organization that repairs Russian nuclear-powered ships, to sell for $55,000 two pounds of uranium yellowcake, a precurser to HEU.

Pundits often have speculated about what happened to suitcase-sized nuclear bombs made during the closing years of the Cold War. The late Russian general Alexander Lebed claimed, on *60 Minutes* and elsewhere, that many were missing. However, some dismiss his statements as tall tales of a heavy drinker with the reputation of saying what would garner him headlines. All of the portable atomic weapons were supposed to have been dismantled in accordance with a 1991 treaty and under the supervision of American officials from the Department of Energy, but some say they were not.

Various individuals, some nefarious, have bought on Pakistan's black market "nuclear starter kits" with warhead blueprints and enough uranium to make a small bomb. Once a group has thirty pounds of HEU plus readily available design information and equipment, a competent engineer can make a nuclear device within a few months. Articles describing the physics of nuclear weapons and providing schematics are on the Internet. Theodore Taylor, a nuclear physicist who designed both large and small bombs, noted that with fissile material building a bomb is "very easy. Double underline. Very easy."

Means: Thirty thousand trucks, six thousand five hundred rail cars, and one hundred forty ships deliver more than fifty thousand cargo containers into the United States every day, but only 5 percent of the containers are ever screened—and even that screening might not detect nuclear weapons or material. With an estimated twenty thousand pounds of cocaine and marijuana smuggled into the United States each day, it wouldn't be hard to smuggle in a softball-sized thirty pounds of HEU. One hundred pounds of it plus all the other parts of a bomb would fit easily into the back of an SUV or some other similarly nondescript delivery vehicle.

In 2003 ABC News placed a lead-lined pipe containing depleted uranium inside a Samsonite suitcase that was then stored inside a teak trunk and shipped through an ordinary freight forwarding company from Indonesia to Los Angeles. The trunk made it to Los Angeles without any trouble. Customs officials are upgrading port security, but progress has been slow. The easiest way to bring a nuclear weapon into the United States is probably in a cargo container by sea.

The porous United States–Mexico border could also be the pathway for bringing in a bomb, but others argue that terrorists who do not bring in a bomb by ship would be best served by coming in through Canada. Author Richard Miniter noted that many major Canadian cities have significant Muslim immigrant populations, making it easier for al Qaeda members to blend in, and that al Qaeda manuals instruct members of terrorist cells in Western countries to get on welfare so they can work full-time on terrorism. Canada has a generous welfare system; essentially Mexico does not.

Furthermore, Canadian police officers who arrest a suspected terrorist may come under press assault for racial or ethnic prejudice, being called racist or worse; prosecutors and judges are also reluctant to take on terrorist cases. As a result, Miniter wrote, "Canada's law enforcement treats terrorists the way its fishermen treat trout: 'catch and release.'"

Motive: One of Osama bin Laden's press mouthpieces, Sulaiman Abu Ghaith, has announced that al Qaeda aspires "to kill four million Americans, including one million children," in response to casualties purportedly inflicted on Muslims by the United States and Israel. Alternately, Israel could be the first target of a Muslim terrorist nuclear bomb, although al Qaeda might have concern about winds wafting a radiation plume into predominantly Muslim territory. Russia, given its long battle with Chechnya, might also be the primary target.

LIKELY RESULTS

The 9/11 Commission Report detailed the problems in response time of large governmental bureaucracies and concluded, "Once the danger has fully materialized, evident to all, mobilizing action is easier—but it then may be too late." If those with material, means, and motive brought a bomb into the United States, what would be the result, and is there any way to stop an explosion from happening?

We can start by realizing that a ten-kiloton bomb exploding at the Smithsonian (the Hiroshima bomb was a twelve-kiloton) would destroy everything from the White House to the Capitol building, with uncontrollable fires raging all the way to the Pentagon. In other cities as well, every body and building up to one-third of a mile from the epicenter would vanish, and everything up to one and one-half miles away would be destroyed by fires and radiation. A report in 2003 by the Energy Department's National Nuclear Security Administration estimated that a Washington, D.C., nuclear explosion could kill three hundred thousand persons. A report in 2004 by the Homeland Security Council (HSC) used different assumptions and came up with a number of "only" one hundred thousand.

Furthermore, those exposed to substantial radiation would develop an acute radiation sickness that seriously damages tissue. Those who showed no symptoms would have an increased risk of eventually developing cancer. Other damage would come from a nuclear weapon's electromagnetic pulse, which would destroy all electronic circuitry, including that in computers, cars, and communications equipment. The HSC report noted that it would take years to clean up three to five thousand square miles around a nuclear explosion, with many irradiated neighborhoods simply abandoned. A nuclear attack "would forever change the American psyche, its politics and worldview."

It would be difficult to detect a lead-shielded nuclear device, since radiation detectors now in use in some major cities would probably not detect a lead-shielded nuclear device. Nuclear Energy Support Teams (NESTs), sometimes called volunteer fire departments for the atomic age, could be rapidly deployed to assess risks, find nuclear weapons, and disarm them, but only in movies are they likely to be successful. The goal has to be to learn about terrorist plans through intelligence work, including wiretaps and other surveillance methods, and stop bomb plots before they are close to fruition.

Terrorists kept from getting their hands on or exploding a nuclear weapon have a fallback position: a "dirty bomb" made of ordinary explosives wrapped together with a morsel of radioactive material. An explosion from one of these bombs in a crowded area could kill several thousand and make at least several square miles of prime real estate unusable. A cobalt radiation bomb exploded in Manhattan could require the evacuation of the entire island, with people unable to come back safely for months.

The economic consequences of even a dirty bomb would be large, and the psychological consequences enormous. The anthrax scare late in 2001, like the Katrina disaster in 2005, led to panic and outrage about problems small in relation to those that would result from any kind of nuclear explosion. Terrorists undoubtedly relish the thoughts of wreaking such havoc, so it is remarkable that we haven't already had some kind of nuclear disaster. Interviewers for two years have asked Graham Allison why we have not had one, and his regular answer has been, "It's a great puzzle." He said, "I think that we should be very thankful that it hasn't happened already. . . . We're living on borrowed time."

The Bush administration may have won us some time. Early on it recognized the danger in what Vice President Cheney called the "nexus between terrorists and weapons of mass destruction." It toppled the Taliban in Afghanistan and Saddam Hussein's regime in Iraq, both made up of people willing and ready to give terrorists sanctuary and the opportunity to plan disaster in peace. The Bush administration, by showing it was not tame, also made it less likely that North Korea or Iran would give nuclear weapons to terrorists, because those leaders could suspect that their countries would be incinerated if a nuclear attack on the United States was traced back to them.

The lack of an incident from September 12, 2001, through the completion of this book (June 2006) is still difficult to explain. After all, all a terrorist organization needs is for one band to get through; others are expendable. Terrorists could also introduce panic by means other than explosions: a subtler attack would be biological, probably using anthrax, botulism, smallpox, or plague. We would not be aware of the attack until several days after release of the agent; only after masses of individuals became sick and required treatment would the role of terrorism become evident.

With so much going wrong, the lack of terrorist attacks is an indication that something is right in the world.

Chapter 17

PANDEMIC

Epidemics were once a regular part of American culture. The New Orleans 1853 yellow fever epidemic officially killed 7,848 persons. Twenty-five years later yellow fever again killed 3,977 in New Orleans and 5,150 in Memphis. *Leslie's Weekly* described one family in a room, the mother dead "with her body sprawled across the bed . . . black vomit like coffee grounds spattered all over . . . the children rolling on the floor, groaning."

Over the years, though, medicine has made enormous progress in the battle against epidemics and pandemics. Researchers and pharmaceutical companies have conquered smallpox, polio, diphtheria, and the like. The United States has not had a flu pandemic since 1918. It was a bad one, killing more than twice as many people as died in the world war just concluding, and it moved quickly, with one hospital finding that the time from admission to death was about half a day: "It is simply a struggle for air until they suffocate. It is horrible. One can stand it to see one, two or twenty men die, but to see these poor devils dropping like flies . . ."

But we have not had disasters like that since, only false alarms like the one in 1976 when some predicted that one million Americans would die from swine flu. Emergency inoculations began, and the threat fizzled. So have others. We hear occasional mentions of a new fear, avian flu, but the World Health Organization notes that Scottish chickens had the current variety (H5N1) in 1959, English turkeys in 1991, and Hong Kong chickens in 1997. In all that time it has not mutated so that a human who catches it from a bird can pass it on to another human. Headlines in 1997 hyped the "Race to Prevent World Epidemic of Lethal 'Bird Flu,'" but that also was a false alarm.

The latest overhyped health menace came in fall 2004, when mistakes by a flu vaccine maker left the United States with only sixty million doses of vaccine against the flu expected that year. Reporters trumpeted the dreaded word "shortage," suggested that getting a shot was a life or death issue (which it can be for the very old or the very ill), and thereby created a temporary shortage. Even though the sixty million doses were enough for a normal year, anxious people soon were spending hours in line waiting for a shot. It turned out there were enough doses for everyone who wanted one, but the experience showed how concerned Americans are about health risks. Since we pity more the soldier who dies on the last day of a war rather than in the middle of it ("He was so close to safety"), the elimination of many diseases seems to have left us more anxious about those that remain.

THE NEW THREAT

Public anxiety grew again during 2005 as avian flu began to rage among birds in China and other East Asian countries. The numbers are enormous: in recent years China's domesticated fowl population has leaped from twelve million to thirteen billion. Lack of hygiene contributes to the onset of diseases: most U.S. chickens are raised indoors and rarely come in contact with the wild birds that spread bird flu, but in Asia many people live in close proximity to outdoor chicken flocks. By the end of the year, chickens throughout Asia and also in Eastern Europe had come down with the disease, and scattered cases appeared in Africa.

Dr. Klaus Stohr of the World Health Organization's Global Influenza Program was one of many to look at the period since the last pandemic and think that the world is due: "Somebody calculated that every twenty-seven years a pandemic occurs, on average. The last one was thirty-six years ago. So we are somewhat beyond the odds." He said that the best-case scenario for a soon-to-arrive flu pandemic would be two to seven million deaths around the world.

Sometimes lost in the shuffling were the odds against the pandemic. Most avian viruses cannot be transmitted to humans: that's because the receptor proteins in bird and human lungs are very different. The hemagglutinin protein of the H5N1 virus binds easily to bird cells, allowing the virus to replicate easily, but struggles in human cells. Viruses constantly drift and shift, so H5N1 could swap chunks of genetic code with human influenza and become something that could pass from person to person like a common cold does, but that's not probable. A pandemic would emerge only if there were widespread human-to-human transmission of the virus, but in December 2005, neither the World Health Organization in Geneva nor Shu Yuelong, director of China's national influenza laboratory, saw any evidence of that.

Still no U.S. official after Katrina wants to be caught underestimating dangers, so the Department of Health and Human Services offered a worst-case scenario if a pandemic occurs: two million Americans would die, with panicky people overwhelming hospitals, fighting for food, and rioting at vaccination clinics. The HHS scenario also has ninety-three million people becoming ill at some point during the sixteen prime weeks of the pandemic, with eight and a half million people hospitalized, and costs exceeding $450 billion.

The Congressional Budget Office chimed in with its worst-case financial cost: $675 billion. Some said these big numbers, based on the 1918 historical parallel, are hysterical because an H5N1 pandemic, were one to emerge, would not be a replay of 1918. We now have antivirals, antibiotics, and vaccines against many types of pneumococcal bacteria; not the flu itself but secondary complications, particularly pneumonia, caused the huge death total.

Some scientists also suspected that H5N1 had far less than the 50 percent fatality rate initially feared, since many people infected might have only minor symptoms. Others noted, though, that the existence of many undetected cases might create greater opportunity for the virus to mutate.

Was technology friend or foe? The good news was that improved communications since 1918 would give us warning and time to prepare. The bad news was that worldwide air travel would quickly spread the disease. The two-day typical influenza incubation period—the time from infection to visible illness—would allow those infected to transmit the virus during the day before they become ill. It's likely that the typical person becoming ill would transmit the virus to two or three other persons. Pessimists argue that the medical system would be quickly overwhelmed, with the improvements of nearly nine decades not making a difference for most victims.

President Bush, in April 2005, mused about the matter at a press conference: "The policy decisions for a president in dealing with an avian flu outbreak are difficult. One example: if we had an outbreak somewhere in the United States, do we not then quarantine that part of the country, and how do you then enforce a quarantine?" The question was a good one, since quarantines in a land of individualism are hard to maintain. The HHS Pandemic Influenza Plan informs us that state, local, and tribal authorities "should be able to" isolate individuals and then set up voluntary quarantine measures. But that plan reads like some hurricane disaster plans, filled with generalities and good intentions but light on specifics.

LIKELY RESULTS

Again, an avian flu pandemic is unlikely—but if it did arise and come to the United States, it would probably last for six to eight weeks, with two weaker waves following in subsequent months. Once under way, it would be like Heisman Trophy winner Reggie Bush during the 2005 football season: you can't stop it, so your only hope is to contain it. The number of people to die would depend on the virulence of the mutated flu, but it clearly would produce economic disaster: perhaps no air travel for a much longer time than after 9/11. Interstate commerce could decline enormously for a time. Millions of people could be without outside supplies for not days but weeks.

The HHS Pandemic Influenza Plan notes the problems but, after four hundred pages of discussion, still leaves it unclear as to whether or how food and other supplies would be delivered, what would happen with jobs and schooling—many little details like that. The Pandemic Influenza Plan emphasizes the need for "timely and transparent dissemination of clear, accurate, science-based, culturally competent information about pandemic influenza, and the progress of the response can build public trust and confidence." It offers good intentions but no specifics. Based on Katrina reporting, it's likely that the media would spread panic.

Reporting of pandemic plans, so far, has also been short on detail, but that may be inevitable given our difficulty in coming to grips with such threats. In one broadcast CBS medical reporter Sanjay Gupta said, "There might be recommended isolation. . . . You might be told on your local news or even [by] a phone call or something to stay home, don't be outside, stockpile some food and don't come in contact with people until we tell you. And I think that's going to be some of the most effective measures." Really? After the experience of Katrina in New Orleans, do we really think that all or even most people will stockpile food, and that they will obey instructions?

Given how dire a pandemic could be, it's logical to ask whether public policy steps taken in advance could reduce its likelihood. The traditional way of stopping the spread of H5N1 among birds had been to destroy poultry exposed to the virus: in Asia and eastern Europe, about one hundred fifty million birds had died or been killed by the end of 2005 in an effort to stop the virus. But stopping the spread is also possible through bird inoculation, and at the end of 2005 China announced a national plan to inoculate its poultry for H5N1.

Many people in the United States also favor such inoculations—and with the poultry vaccine, the problem at the end of 2005 was political, not technological. The U.S. Department of Agriculture had stockpiled forty million doses of poultry vaccine for four strains of bird flu and, in December 2005, was seeking funds from Congress to acquire seventy million more, largely to protect poultry from H5N1. A crew of seven or eight workers wearing protective gear would inject vaccine into the necks of chickens, taking a week to treat a typical farm holding about one hundred thousand birds. The cost would be about $500 million for enough vaccine to inoculate all of America's ten billion chickens, and another $500 million for labor.

A politically potent opposition to vaccination was coming from the National Chicken Council, a trade association representing companies such as Tyson Foods and Perdue Farms, which said vaccination would hurt the $2 billion chicken export business. The poultry industry said that major importers of U.S. chickens would not accept vaccinated poultry, since the basic screening tests that they use for bird flu can't determine for sure whether chickens have been infected or vaccinated. They also noted one reason not to vaccinate poultry: massive deaths among unvaccinated chickens would serve as a warning that the virus had arrived.

The poultry industry said it has other ways to fight a chicken pandemic: kill all the chickens in an area around an infected group, require workers and visitors to wear protective clothing, and so forth. But the major concern is dollars, and if a refusal to spend contributes to a pandemic among humans, the love of money will have contributed to a slaughter that would justifiably result in the most bitter of recriminations.

CREATING A VACCINE

The human vaccine question sits amid a different economic and legal landscape. Since viruses frequently mutate, a vaccine often works for only one season, so a manufacturer must recover its entire cost of production in a few months. The movie business is somewhat analogous in its emphasis on fast recovery of investment—the first weekend of theater exhibition is key—except that movies have DVD sales. But no one wants a vaccine past its prime.

Furthermore, even if a proven vaccine were available, production of it in massive quantities would take at least six months from the appearance of the particular pandemic-causing strain. That's because we still depend on a sixty-year-old process for producing vaccines from fertilized eggs. Some politicians have been calling for the production of six hundred million vaccines within six months, which is more than ten times current capacity: those intentions are good, but six months would not be fast enough. We need a breakthrough—a genetically engineered universal flu vaccine would be ideal, and whoever comes up with it deserves both fame and fortune.

Progress has been slow, perhaps because of technical difficulties, but also due to forced low-cost licensing and the prospect of litigation. To understand the licensing problem, imagine that if a movie became hugely popular, governments would suddenly declare it illegal to charge eight dollars to see it; to insure that poor people were not excluded, theaters would be allowed to charge only a dime. To understand the litigation threat, imagine that filmmakers could lose all their profits and possibly the entire company if a few viewers had negative reactions to the product on screen.

Now, let's turn from entertainment to life-and-death matters. Doctors at the end of 2005 believed that the antiviral drug Tamiflu, if taken within forty-eight hours of avian flu onset, would be able to relieve the worst symptoms and prevent many deaths. (Tamiflu did not help two avian flu victims in Vietnam, but that appeared to have been an isolated occurrence.) The Swiss company Roche should have been receiving glory, laud, and money for bringing the drug to the world. Instead, Roche faced calls to sell Tamiflu or license government production of it in many countries at practically giveaway prices, and risked being labeled a mass murderer if it requested a return on its investment.

At the end of 2005, the World Health Organization was trying to force Roche to give up its Tamiflu patent rights; officials in Indonesia, Taiwan, and other countries had forced Roche to license production; and New York Senator Charles Schumer was among the American politicians proposing that the United States break Roche's patent rights. Many agreed on the goal—the rapid production of Tamiflu—but few noted that mandating production at confiscatory prices would send a negative message to researchers and companies deciding whether to invest heavily in developing drugs that could preserve life from the next threats.

It was vital to produce more Tamiflu but to do so in a way that gave Roche a good return on its investment. Although it's risky business to use an avian metaphor when discussing bird flu, politicians were lining up to strangle a goose that laid a golden egg. They could win immediate popularity by letting people get drugs more cheaply. Few had eyes to see what does not yet exist—and what will not unless inventors receive encouragement. Nor did many politicians care: the pandemic a decade or two down the road will not be on their watch and will not affect their immediate electoral chances. They could be vote-wise and life-foolish: their breaking of the seventh commandment ("Do not steal") could lead regularly to their breaking of the sixth ("Do not murder").

Strangling this goose is a bird-brained idea. Bill Gates, whose foundation is helping health programs around the world, noted that the key issue in increasing world health isn't the cost of drugs but "the drugs that aren't being invented, and part of the reason they aren't being invented is that [if] the pharmaceutical companies work in these areas, then they're expected to give the drugs away." There are two better ways: either pay market prices for needed drugs or offer big prizes for companies that come up with vital drugs. George Mason University economist Tyler Cowan suggested that the federal government offer Roche the option of licensing production in this country at generous prices and with favorable regulatory treatment and easy facility construction.

LITIGATION, AGAIN

Licensing issues are one part of the problem; legal liability questions also need answers. The litigation threat is one that has grown over the past half century, during which time the number of vaccine makers in the United States shrank from twenty-six in 1957 to four, with two of the four doing little in vaccine research. We have vaccine shortages in nine of the twelve vaccines commonly given to children. The problem is that when a large population is vaccinated, a small percentage (but a large number) will become ill, and almost all will be approached by lawyers who say big bucks are waiting.

The legal path could be cleared if courts did not impose strict liability for rare side effects but instead required proof of negligence. Alternatively, the federal government could indemnify vaccine manufacturers for damages attributed to the vaccine. The National Vaccine Injury Compensation Program, since its creation in 1986, has done that for rare injuries sustained following the administering of vaccines used routinely for children. However, it does not cover many vaccines, does not cover unborn children, and gives gambling lawyers the option of going before juries that sometimes run away from both law and science. These holes need to be plugged so that predatory lawsuits do not force companies to decide between their own survival and the public interest.

Overall, in our avoidance of risk, we've created or sustained FDA regulations tougher than those of western Europe and in the process provided a tad more safety at the cost of innovation: to use a football metaphor, our game plan has given us 6–3 rather than 42–7 wins, and allowed officials to boast that we allowed no touchdowns. This is an inadequate metaphor when the price of an innovation that saves thousands is the loss of an innocent life, but the fight against disease is a war. Officers who write letters to grieving mothers know how difficult it is to lose anyone, but in war some soldiers die that more may triumph.

On these life-or-death matters, the politics of disaster have pushed us to try to get by on the cheap. Federal procurers have been efficient in this one area: since the U.S. government is the largest purchaser of vaccines used for children, it has been able to pay low prices in a penny-wise but life-foolish way. The government should pay higher prices for vaccines or, if the government-pressured marketplace will not provide a high enough return to attract companies to jump in, it should offer substantial prizes for innovation.

Licensing and litigation questions are difficult not logically but politically; when some politicians tire of making threats about gasoline prices, they assault pharmaceutical companies. And yet Paul Offit, chief of infectious diseases at the Children's Hospital of Philadelphia, pointed out that these companies should be honored: during the past century they have been the major contributor to increasing the American lifespan by thirty years. They created and mass-produced vaccines against pertussis (whooping cough) that dropped the number of children's deaths from eight thousand annually to fewer than twenty, vaccines against polio that reduced the number of children it paralyzed annually from fifteen thousand to zero, and vaccines against rubella (German measles) that reduced the number of children with severe birth defects from twenty thousand to zero.

Removing litigation disincentives to mass production is particularly important because we may not be far off from some vital breakthroughs in vaccine production. Scientists are beginning to genetically engineer viruses that could be used in vaccines. One company plans to use canine cultures to produce avian flu vaccine. Overall, it looks like the time to produce a vaccine could be cut from six months or more to three months or less. Companies are also working to use less of a vaccine supply by mixing in adjuvants, chemicals that magnify vaccine effects so that what was needed for one dose can now cover forty or fifty.

Those advances could come soon, but now, as HHS secretary Mike Leavitt said near the end of 2005, "We are underprepared." That is not surprising, because politicians who gain votes by concentrating on what produces immediate results tend to be "Chicken Bigs," suggesting that since the sky did not fall during the swine flu pandemic or during other times of warning, it won't fall this time either. Since we are always surrounded by risks of low probability, since it's hard to know which carries the greatest emergency, and since the likelihood of any particular disaster hitting during the term of office is small, underpreparedness is standard.

NEW ORLEANS WRIT LARGE?

And so we are left with the possibility of a national New Orleans. If food distribution were to falter while many people stayed sequestered, the chaos rumored in New Orleans would become reality in every major city. With distribution costs increasing and scarcities common, prices for food and other essential goods could soar. Some jobs would disappear, job absenteeism would grow, mortgage defaults would increase, and the threat of bank runs and closures would be great. Probably every company in the airline industry would go into bankruptcy. The Federal Reserve would need to be prepared to increase liquidity in financial markets and keep check-clearing systems from shutting down.

Here's where sector-by-sector planning is crucial. Maintaining electric power would be important, so utilities should plan to have crews of technicians—especially those without families—living at power stations to improve the prospects of continuity of supply. It would be vital to keep open ports to receive shipments of oil and gas and transport them to refineries. Since schools would close during a pandemic, teachers would need to be prepared to post work online and do virtual instruction. Some companies plan to have employees work from home should disaster approach, which makes sense not only to avoid spreading the virus but also because day-care centers would be closed.

Local health care systems would be stretched and stressed as never before, so they would need to have and use databases of volunteers—doctors, nurses, other professionals—willing to help out in case a pandemic hits. With emergency rooms crowded by flu patients, it would be important to turn church halls and school gyms into clinics for those with nonflu emergency medical needs. Medical facilities would have to have stockpiled testing kits for avian flu and large supplies of antibiotics, respirators, IV fluids, and the other innovations that can make a new pandemic much less costly in lives than the 1918 disaster. Generic statin drugs used to fight cholesterol might also fight the secondary results of flu infection.

Let's look at how each of the major players would function at the peak of a pandemic. The military would not be needed for riot control operations because most people would avoid crowds, unless utter desperation came. Companies such as FedEx would be crucial in shipping as other patterns of commerce broke down. Faith-based organizations would be crucial both in direct relief work and in the preservation of community when everything seemed chaotic. But individual action, from stockpiling food before the crisis to frequent hand washing and mask wearing during it, would be essential.

So preparation is important, but we should not obsess over avian flu at the expense of other medical issues. The next pandemic or public health crisis could come from any number of sources, so we should focus on local preparedness and flexibility in responding to surprises, whether they result from terrorism or natural catastrophes. With all the threats out there, we should remember that we are not living in exceptionally dangerous times. In premodern times most children died during their first five years of life. In modern times, every generation has faced massive hazards: for example, Americans, in December 1941, found themselves facing both Nazi Germany and militant Japan, and averted disaster by becoming "the greatest generation."

During the Cold War, the USSR pointed nuclear missiles at the United States and seemed poised to use them. For years disaster seemed imminent and leaders were sometimes erratic; for example, in the most famous near-catastrophe of them all, the Cuban Missile Crisis of 1962, a man famous for shoe-banging rages and vodka drinking led the Soviet Union, and a president on amphetamines led the United States. (A doctor who treated John F. Kennedy and warned him about amphetamine use observed, "No president with his finger on the red button has any business taking stuff like that.")

Kennedy's favorite literary line was from Shakespeare's *Henry IV*, part 1, where Glendower brags, "I can call spirits from the vasty deep," and Hotspur responds, "Why, so can I, or so can any man; but will they come when you do call for them?" Kennedy's nuclear demons would come if he called, and Khruschev had similar power. White House officials discussed ways of keeping Soviet missile bases in Cuba from becoming operative: A U.S. invasion of Cuba? A quick U.S. air attack on the bases? A blockade of Soviet ships?

They decided on the blockade, and it worked—but it could have ended tragically, and so could have many other confrontations. Might God have preserved us? It's wise in studying history to look for natural explanations of events and to consider the supernatural only when the natural seem thoroughly unlikely. But anyone in 1945 could have received tremendously favorable odds for a wager that, during the next sixty years, the most potent weapon in the armaments of enemy countries would remain unused. Our delivery from that evil might give us hope that we will be delivered from others.

Chapter 18

BEYOND WORRY

Do not be anxious about your life. . . . Look at the birds of the air: they neither sow nor reap nor gather into barns, and yet your heavenly Father feeds them. Are you not of more value than they? And which of you by being anxious can add a single hour to his span of life?" (Matt. 6:26–27).

These words from Christ's Sermon on the Mount stand against fear of major disasters plus an endless list of potential hazards, from killer bees to falling airline debris hitting hazardous waste sites and scattering toxic chemicals everywhere. But how can we not worry, especially when presidents tell us that the number of disasters keeps increasing? Again, look at the numbers of disaster and emergency declarations: from thirteen a year during the Eisenhower administration to twenty-eight per year under Reagan, eighty-eight per year under Clinton, and one hundred thirty-six per year under George W. Bush (first term).

We tend to maintain an "it can't happen here" arrogance and continue our building plans, but at the same time embrace fatalistic attitudes: "If it happens here, it happens." Fatalism breeds lassitude, but it may also lead to insolence. If actions do not matter, a runner who could make second base might just as well stay at first, and a runner who has almost no chance of stealing home might as well go for it and be tagged out. Political fatalists want government to do nothing or government to make all things right. Some political fatalists give up, and others prance before network cameras and confuse themselves with King Canute, decreeing that the ocean waves must pause.

A better perspective regarding disaster might keep us from plopping down billions for new buildings below sea level. A better perspective suggests taking prudent risks and not fearing change. Fatalism was a staple of Greek and Roman beliefs and still figures prominently in Hinduism (karma), Islam (kismet), and many tribal religions, but it never has been part of biblical thinking, which historically emphasizes the concept of providence. Maybe we need to reawaken that understanding if we are to deal with disasters in ways neither foolhardy nor fearful.

FATALISM VS. PROVIDENCE

A story about one of Stonewall Jackson's aides, Presbyterian minister Robert L. Dabney, illustrates the contrast between fatalism and providence. One day in 1862 Dabney preached a sermon on God's "special providence," noting that in a recent battle, "every shot and shell and bullet was directed by the God of battles." Not much later Dabney found himself under fire and took cover behind a large gatepost. A nearby officer kidded him: "If the God of battles directs every shot, why do you want to put a gatepost between you and a special providence?" Dabney replied, "Just here the gatepost is the special providence."

The contrast between fatalism and providence is also clear in sports, in which victories depend on players stepping up when their team is behind rather than resignedly going through the motions. Johnny Oates, the former Texas Rangers manager who lost his life through cancer in 2004, said,

"We play aggressively; I never want any Christian to be passive and start saying, 'It's God will.' Our goal is to do everything in our power that's not morally wrong or illegal to win a ballgame. Second, if we lose, I tell the players, 'Go look at yourself in the mirror. If you did everything you could, go home and get a good night's rest. If not, remember what you did wrong, then go home and rest.'"

The concept of providence is based on the idea that God rules the world but we don't know outcomes until they occur. It leads brave people to take action when they see children about to die, either physically or psychologically: only when we've done all we can and failed do we know that a death was ordained. Ted Yamamori, former head of the Christian relief agency Food for the Hungry, once described an African woman who was mourning the death of her child. The youngster was sick but still alive, yet the mother was convinced that fate decreed her child's death. Yamamori changed fate by getting the child medicine that restored him to health.

In a similar way, a home with parents who are patient and compassionate can save children abandoned by their birth parents. A fatalist might say that such troubled children are fated to a life of misery, but an adoptive father and mother can become their protecting gateposts and change their lives. The same goes for the victims of disaster, both societal and individual. For example, when Jerod Montague of Clio, Michigan, now in his thirties, was born with cerebral palsy, some could have spoken of fate, but Jerod's father, Jim, internalized Christ's teaching about the man born blind so that God could be glorified. Montague used the profits from a manufacturing company he owned to build next to his own home a $2 million home with room for Jerod and eight others with cerebral palsy. In that way he assisted not only his own son but also the children of others.

The home's mission statement reads: "We believe God doesn't make mistakes. . . . It is a high calling to provide quality care to those physically and mentally challenged in such a way that would be pleasing and honoring to our Heavenly Father and bring emotional and spiritual healing to those who brought them into this world." What if we applied that attitude to helping those who suffered through Katrina or will suffer through the disasters that come? Then every challenge truly becomes an opportunity.

Theological views influence post-Katrina policy choices. Those who say that New Orleans residents got what they deserved because of "their sin" are unlikely to have an interest in helping. Those who say they are merely innocent victims are unlikely to put much stress on the opportunity for change that a catastrophe brings. Both types of fatalism drown hope and keep those who need help from embracing opportunity. Christians come to understand that even an immense personal disaster may not be what it first appears. One well-known author, Joni Eareckson Tada, was immersed as a teenager in meaninglessness until she dove into shallow water and broke her neck. She felt her life was over, but her true life was just beginning, as her paralysis eventually led her to Christ and to proclamation of a testimony that has inspired millions of others.

The authors of the Bible frequently reported on disasters and described them as coming from God, yet at the same time referred to the disaster-bringer as our Father. The metaphor is important: a good father does not protect his children from all injuries, and God does not protect his children from all suffering. He knows his children need to make decisions and see the repercussions of those decisions, or they will never become mature. When we substitute government for God, though, we obtain a father who fluctuates wildly from overprotection to malign neglect, and rarely gets it right.

C. S. Lewis noted in *The Problem of Pain* (HarperSanFrancisco, 2001), "The problem of reconciling human suffering with the existence of a God who loves is insoluble only so long as we attach a trivial meaning to the word 'love.'" This suggests that the problem of theodicy—how can a good God bring about suffering?—is not a problem: God could not be a good father if he kept his creatures from all hardship. This means that the real difficulty is not "the problem of suffering," but the problem of what we as humans feel is excess suffering in terms of what we perceive to be gained. And yet, do we have a better perspective on that than God has?

BIBLICAL DISASTER REPORTING

The Puritans had many faults (including at times a pride in their ability to acknowledge the sin of pride), but their understanding of disaster reflected the biblical perspective. Increase Mather wrote, "However we may be diminished and brought low through Oppression, Affliction, and Sorrow, yet our God will have compassion on us. [His] design, in bringing the Calamity upon us, is not to destroy us but to humble us, and reform us, and to do us good." Today's journalists could look at the way Mather's contemporaries, and those who came shortly after, reported the disasters of their era.

For example, a 1684 London broadsheet about a blizzard tried to convey the imminence of disaster without losing a sense of the transcendence. The news report began:

> As Passengers along the Rode did go
> The North-east wind most bitterly did blow
> And flakes of Snow did from the Heavens fall
> As if it meant destruction unto all. . . .
> Two Passengers that were both Man and Wife
> In this extremity did part with life
> It would have griev'd a stony heart to see't
> How these poor souls lay starved feet to feet. . . .
> And thirty more in Sometshire were lost
> In this unusual Snow and cruel Frost
> Who little thought when they went out of door
> Their wives & children to see no more.

The author then offered specific detail: "For the better satisfaction of the incredulous, I here insert the Names of several who have sufficiently tasted of the bitterness of this outrageous Storm and Frost, and are yet alive to testify the Verity thereof." But his major point was the presence of sin, not among those who died—nowhere is there the sense that God picked out those specific victims for punishment—but among all:

> Our sins for vengeance do to Heaven cry
> Yet we like sinners live in vanity

> O grant that we our sinful lives may mend
> That we may live with thee when life doth end.

During the following century, when the most destructive earthquake ever recorded in the eastern United States struck thirty miles north of Boston, reporting was similar. This 1755 quake damaged more than one thousand houses in the Boston area and sent one hundred chimneys falling into the street. A broadsheet quickly reported the news and its significance:

> While God sends forth his thundering Voice
> And bids the Earth to quake
> Let Men attend the Sovereign Sound
> And all the Nations wake.

The report did not point fingers but noted the presence of the sin that all shared:

> In Depth of Sleep, or Scenes of Guilt
> Sinners securely lay
> When sudden shook the tott'ring Ground
> And threatened to give way. . . .
> Around them crack their shatter'd Walls
> The Beams and Timber creak
> And the Inhabitants amaz'd
> With dismal Out-crys shriek.

The writer emphasized mercy:

> How thankful should New-England be
> To God our high Support
> So many dreadful Earthquakes felt
> In Life and Limb unhurt.

God's mercy would affect an outpouring of compassion among His followers:

> From Love to him, obey his Law
> Love God with Love supreme
> And as you'd have your Neighbor do
> To you, do you to him.

The substance and style of journalism today is obviously different, but we should pay attention to the question asked in a Virginia news sermon delivered also in 1755: "Are all our affairs under the management of chance?" Pastor Samuel Davies said no and criticized pridefulness in his congregation: "You who can eat, and forget God: you who enjoy the blessing of the sun and rain, and the fruits of the earth, and yet go on as thoughtless of your divine Benefactor as the cattle of your stall, or who look upon these as things of course, or the fruits of your own industry . . . you are practical atheists." For Davies, man's basic sin was arrogance, and disasters were a reminder that all of us depend on God. The pastor's recurrent plea following catastrophe was that we examine ourselves and help those in need.

The *Boston Recorder*'s coverage of the Aleppo, Syria, earthquake of 1822 conveyed a similar message. The *Recorder* included a first-person report: "Men and women clinging to the ruined walls of their houses, holding their children in their trembling arms; mangled bodies lying under my feet, and piercing cries of half buried people assailing my ears; Christians, Jews, and Turks were imploring the Almighty's mercy in their respective tongues, who a minute before did not perhaps acknowledge him." The *Recorder* then turned readers' attention from Syria to home by asking a hard question: "Must we tempt God to visit us also with an earthquake?" The *Recorder* urged its readers to acknowledge the pridefulness of all, not just the victims, and send aid to the suffering.

That's good advice for us as well. Can we be content to understand that we are part of a great story with lots of twists and turns? Nineteenth-century pastor Charles Spurgeon put it this way: "Providence is wonderfully intricate.

Ah! You want always to see through Providence, do you not? You never will, I assure you. You have not eyes good enough. You want to see what good that affliction was to you; you must believe it. You want to see how it can bring good to the soul; you may be enabled in a little time, but you cannot see it now; you must believe it. Honor God by trusting him."

The Bible says God ordains everything that happens, but it also says we are responsible for our actions. Christians have many ways to hash through this, but what appeals to me is this: for God all times are the present. He knows and ordains past and future, while we know only a little about the past and nothing about the future. So even if we are saying lines, they are fresh to us as we are saying them: we are actors without a script, deciding moment by moment from our subjective perspective the direction of the play, even if from God's perspective it is already objectively decided. In all our consciousness we freely decide, choosing from moment to moment what to say and how to act.

Few people today suggest that some of the threats we face—earthquake, terrorism, pandemic—should bring joy. But we should realize that stressful challenge also brings opportunity, for nothing calls more on both our bodies and our brains than responding to disaster. Novelist and Christian existentialist Walker Percy offered a series of pointed questions in his book of essays, *The Message in the Bottle* (Picador, 1975): "Why do people often feel bad in good environments and good in bad environments? . . . Why is a man apt to feel bad in a good environment, say suburban Short Hills, New Jersey, on an ordinary Wednesday afternoon? Why is the same man apt to feel good in a very bad environment, say an old hotel on Key Largo during a hurricane?"

Percy mock-proposed an academic study with the title "Catastrophe as Catalyst in the Ontology of Joy, or Hurricane Parties on the Gulf Coast during Hurricane Camille." There's not much joy in catastrophe, but Dorothy Sayers, in *The Whimsical Christian* (Macmillan, 1978), called Christianity the only religion that gives value to suffering by affirming the reality of suffering and the opportunity to wrench some good out of it, as Christ did when he died for all who believe in him. Christianity makes the same affirmation from all our personal disasters, and offers the same opportunity.

Many Christians find the idea that God is in charge a cheerful one. (Otherwise, imagine the torment after an accident, where people think that if they hadn't offered a second helping of dessert to a person, delayed by a few minutes and in an accident a few minutes later, a tragedy would not have happened.) G. K. Chesterton wrote that the doctrine of original sin is a cheerful concept, since within it, suffering, failure, and inadequacy arise—neither from blind chance nor necessarily as part of punishment, but as the common lot of humanity.

THE WORK OF CHRIST

What makes all this work is the experience of Christ, who knew what it was to be unjustly tortured and abandoned, to endure overwhelming loss, and to be unjustly killed. The ancient Greeks distinguished between *gnosis* (intellectual knowledge) and *epignosis* (intimate understanding drawn from personal experience). Christians understand that God has both and has always had both, since for him all times are the present. And having drawn near to us, God invites us to draw near to him.

Columnist Peggy Noonan wrote in 2001 about a husband and wife swimming in the ocean when "from nowhere came a shark." She said, "The shark went straight for the woman, opened its jaws. Do you know what the man did? He punched the shark in the head. . . . So the shark let go of his wife and went straight for him. And it killed him. The wife survived to tell the story of what her husband had done. He had tried to deck the shark. I told my friends: That's what a wonderful man is, a man who will try to deck the shark."

The Bible teaches that all of us, because of our sin, should be shark bait. If God were to ignore our sin simply by destroying the shark from afar, we could thank him and venerate him, but would we love him? As it is, Christians say, "What a wonderful God, coming to earth to deck the shark."

Joachim Neander's children were the victims of a fatal crash over three centuries ago. He wrote a hymn still sung today, "Praise to the Lord," that includes the line, "How oft in grief hath not He brought thee relief, spreading His wings to o'er shade thee." The central figure, Christian, in *The Pilgrim's Progress* regularly had grief followed by relief, and that seems to be often what God ordains. Christians learn that if we expect life to go smoothly, we will spend much of it discontented, and we won't come to understand God's mercy.

What's hard to accept is that the road to contentment runs through misery. Christ came to earth not only to die but also to live amid rejection. His horribly painful death on Good Friday took several hours. It was terrible physically, spiritually, and psychologically, but think also of the rejection that occurred during the night before the Crucifixion, and all the rejections that occurred prior to Good Friday—rejections by family, by community, by local religious leaders, by national religious leaders. Those also were painful. Those also were a means to a wonderful end.

Biblically, we can be thankful for difficulties that energize us and also thankful for all the days on which no disaster occurs. Passages in Jeremiah about how "disaster shall be let loose upon all the inhabitants of the land" should make us think about all the days God does not let it loose. We believe that every climate should be like Southern California's, but why shouldn't it be like Tierra del Fuego's? With everything that can go wrong in the world, with hurricanes each year filling most of the letters of the alphabet, it's worth noting not only that a bullet named Katrina hit but also that other bullets missed.

Why should we assume good weather and good health? Why not be thankful for days of clear skies or gentle rains? Why think that the relatively few days of disaster are proof of either atheism or divine malevolence? Why not be thankful that God, as described near the end of the book of Jonah, is a "gracious God and merciful, slow to anger and abounding in steadfast love, and relenting from disaster"?

A NOTE ON SOURCES

This is the first book I've written that is based largely on data from Internet sites, checked for accuracy. Media Web sites and LexisNexis were easily accessible sources for press articles. The government publications I cited are available on Web sites, including those of New Orleans and Louisiana governments and the Department of Homeland Security. My thanks also to Google, which helped me find and cross–check relevant blog postings from late August and early September 2005.

Some specific anecdotes come via *World* reporters Jamie Dean and John Dawson. Papers from two of my University of Texas graduate students, Matt Koschmann and Michelle Mosmeyer, pointed me in the right direction concerning the role of Wal-Mart and other companies. Web sites of some faith-based organizations, particularly the Salvation Army and the Southern Baptist Convention, were helpful. The reporting from South Africa, Namibia, Zambia, Cuba, Chile, and Leesburg, Florida, is my own.

Rutherford Platt's *Disasters and Democracy* (Island Press, 1999) and Mary Comerio's *Disaster Hits Home: New Policy for Urban Housing Recovery* (University of California Press, 1998) were the most useful books I found on disaster and public policy. Graham Allison's *Nuclear Terrorism* (Times Books, 2004) is a good primer on that threat, and Stephen J. Spignesi's *Catastrophe!* (Citadel, 2002) introduced me to some historical disasters outside America.

Finally, a word on the source of this book project: my agent, Mark Sweeney. He brought together W Publishing Group publisher David Moberg and me. My thanks also to the W staff, including my managing editor Thom Chittom, who quickly and accurately moved the manuscript to publication.

INDEX